From Value Pricing to Pricing Value

From Value Pricing to Pricing Value

Using Science, Psychology, and Systems to Attract Higher Paying Clients to Your Accounting Firm

Rhondalynn Korolak

BEP BUSINESS EXPERT PRESS

From Value Pricing to Pricing Value: Using Science, Psychology, and Systems to Attract Higher Paying Clients to Your Accounting Firm

Copyright © Business Expert Press, LLC, 2019.

First published in 2019 by
Business Expert Press, LLC
222 East 46th Street, New York, NY 10017
www.businessexpertpress.com

ISBN-13: 978-1-94999-134-5 (paperback)
ISBN-13: 978-1-94999-135-2 (e-book)

Business Expert Press Managerial Accounting Collection

Collection ISSN: 2152-7113 (print)
Collection ISSN: 2152-7121 (electronic)

Cover and interior design by Exeter Premedia Services Private Ltd., Chennai, India

First edition: 2019

10 9 8 7 6 5 4 3 2 1

Printed in the United States of America.

For my daughter Eden, who has shown me what truly is of real value.

Abstract

Understanding and applying the concept of "Pricing Value" is critical for today's accountants—especially for self-employed accountants, CPAs, and small firms who primarily work with small business clients. This book will reveal how to understand, implement, and master the Pricing Value methodology. It will explain the solid academic research behind this approach, discuss how to avoid common pitfalls, and demonstrate step-by-step how to implement the methodology in a practical and persuasive way.

Keywords

business pricing; accounting; managerial accounting; business accounting; value pricing; pricing value; pricing strategy; fixed fees; hourly rates; time based billing; business pricing; pricing on purpose; psychology of pricing; advisory services; CPA; accountant; chartered accountant; accounting practice

Contents

Testimonials

Lord Chesterfield advised, "A man had better overvalue than undervalue himself. …Whatever real merit you have, other people will discover; and people always magnify their own discoveries, as they lessen those of others." In Pricing Value, Rhondalynn Korolak beautifully expands on this sage advice. Effective and profitable pricing can only materialize by understanding your customer's desired state of the future, and that begins with scope of value, not scope of work. Pricing Value lays out the strategies you need to transform your firm's business model, and create a better future for your customers, employees, and you.

> —Ronald J. Baker, Radio-Show Host, The Soul of Enterprise: Business in the Knowledge Economy, author of the best-selling Implementing Value Pricing: A Radical Business Model for Professional Firms, www.thesoulofenterprise.com, and Chief Value Officer, Armanino LLP

Rhondalynn has written a must-read book in the value pricing (sorry, pricing value) movement. Practical examples abound and they punctuate the quick reading prose. Undoubtedly, this book will help more professionals and firms abandon the dying framework of the billable hour and timesheets. Welcome to the new era – Pricing Value!

> —Ed Kless, Radio-Show Host, the Soul of Enterprise: Business in the Knowledge Economy, Senior Director Sage Accountants Solutions, Senior Fellow VeraSage Institute

Rhondalynn has done an incredible job re-framing the value pricing discussion in her latest book "Pricing Value." Redefining the role of value makes a ton of sense and opens the door for very productive conversations with customers and prospects. Having used value pricing for over 25 years, I found myself to be little more than a novice and walked away with lots of nuggets. Although

the book is written primarily for accountants, it is equally valuable for all
services organizations. I will definitely use and recommend this book.
—Dr. Reginald Thomas Lee PhD, Executive advisor | Author
Strategic Cost Transformation & Lies, Damned Lies, & Cost
Accounting, Management Professor Xavier University—Williams
College of Business, President of Business Dynamics Research,
Senior Fellow VeraSage Institute

Pricing Value is a comprehensive encyclopedia of well thought out pricing
theories, case studies, and practical tips/tricks for any 21st century accountant
that is seriously interested in providing value to their clients and capturing
some of that value for themselves. Fail to read this at your peril.
—John Chisholm B.Juris LLB., Adjunct Professor La Trobe
University Law School, Senior Fellow VeraSage Institute

"For pricing enthusiasts, nothing matches a strong theoretical framework that
is easy to put into practice. For me "Pricing Value" is exactly that and the 150
pages are rich in detail and with many relevant real-life cases… making the
time from reading it to getting the prices you deserve, as short as possible."
—Claus Thorn Madsen MBA, Partner, Implement Consulting
Group, Copenhagen, Denmark

Introduction

It is impossible to attend a conference, read an article, or participate in a social media forum where value pricing is NOT one of the leading topics of conversation among accountants. In fact, many of you have been debating the economic virtues and best practices to implement it for years, if not decades.

Here is the problem—there is a reason why value pricing has been talked about for ages but so few accountants have actually implemented it. Inherent in the phrase "value pricing" is a subtle sleight of hand or misdirection…

The simple structure of the phrase "value pricing" unconsciously predisposes you to focus most of your attention on the word "pricing," and that has been your single biggest mistake. It has inadvertently caused you to waste 90 percent of your time and effort asking unhelpful and dangerous questions such as:

- How many price options should I offer?
- What do I need to do to get my clients to pay more?
- What quoting or proposal apps should I use to help me price my services?
- What if I lose clients or don't make a profit?
- What if my clients are [primarily] price conscious?

And just like that, your value pricing journey turned into a nightmare where everything was "about you," your pricing tactics, and the price you needed to get… Very little time and resources were left to focus on the value (or perceived value) in the eyes of your client. Many of you hesitated in your decision to shift merely because you were worried that you did not know enough, when in reality all you need to do is simply focus on what is of value to your client.

"Pricing Value" is the antidote to this common practice nightmare.

By swapping the two words back to front and placing the emphasis on "value," it focuses you squarely on the maximum value your client is willing to pay based on the Economic Value of the solution to the pain points keeping him/her up at night. It takes the emphasis away from you and the semantics of pricing, and forces you to uncover and quantify the pain points, feelings, and desired transformations that will cause price to become a non-issue, thus leaving your proposed solution as the only sane option.

Pricing Value ensures that both you and your client are focused on their priorities to cure the pain (or achieve their vision of the future), and it deflects the spotlight away from price. It is about helping your clients to see the impact of continuing to ignore the problems (or do nothing), rather than trying to "sell your services or packages" to them.

Now granted, this is a subtle nuance—the word "value" has been dragged to its rightful position of prominence and importance in the phrase. However, the re-ordering of the two words is one that ultimately makes ALL the difference in the world.

Pricing Value ensures that your client is 100 percent engaged and, therefore, motivated to acquire the solution to the problems that have been keeping him/her up at night (or the compelling vision that they have for the future). It achieves the perfect balance of certainty, choice, and cure for your client. And it is compelling and effective because it has been designed based on scientific, psychological, and systems-based research.

What's Changed and Does It Even Matter?

We are in a time of unprecedented transformation. A generation ago, most business owners knew one or two accountants at best. The advent of Google, social media, and online networking has changed buyer behavior radically. Today, everyone is just one or two clicks (i.e., 3.5 degrees of separation) away from finding a new accountant.[1] Pause for a moment, and let the gravity of that sink in. One or two clicks and you can potentially wave goodbye to tens of thousands of dollars' worth of business. That is why Pricing Value matters.

---

[1] Chew, J. 2016. "It's Actually 3.5 Degrees of Separation, Says Facebook." *Fortune*, February 5, 2016, http://fortune.com/2016/02/05/facebook-separation-degrees/

In 2011, Google published The Zero Moment of Truth.[2] It showed that potential clients now contact providers 80 percent of the way into their buyer's journey. This means they will often have researched the market extensively before they ring your firm. As a result, you now have to rethink how you communicate your value proposition and distinguish yourself from your competition during every phase of your relationship with your clients: from the moment they first click on a link in Facebook or LinkedIn, to the point of engagement and onboarding, and throughout each year that you are privileged to work with them.

Social media has also made it easier for clients to share complaints about poor service or excessive prices. When a potential client asks for recommendations on Facebook, would you rather be the firm that basks in the glow of positive client praise, or the one your clients slam with criticism? Unfortunately, if you fail to deliver value for your clients, your firm could easily go viral—but not in a positive way!

Technology sets another challenge for accountants: the automation of compliance. Cloud-based accounting software and apps have streamlined this work, and our clients are wise to it. They are no longer content to pay the same amount as last year for run-of-the-mill accounting or bookkeeping work. The Good, The Bad and the Ugly, a report published in 2017, shows that accountants are now delivering greater value for the same (and in some cases lower) revenue.[3] New Zealand is a world leader when it comes to the adoption of financial technology. As a result, accountants in the Land of the Long White Cloud are already under pressure to lower the prices they charge for compliance work.[4]

In Australia, The National Australia Bank (NAB) recently asked over 750 small businesses what they expected from their accountants.

---

[2] Google & Shopper Sciences. 2011. "The Zero Moment of Truth Macro Study." *Think with Google*, April 2011, https://thinkwithgoogle.com/consumer-insights/the-zero-moment-of-truth-macro-study/

[3] *The Good, the Bad and the Ugly of the Australian Accounting Profession: Benchmarking Report and Practice Improvement Guide for Australian Accounting Firms*, Business Fitness, 2017.

[4] Efrat, Z. 2016. "Top Global Challenges Facing Accounting Practices Today." *In the Black*, November 1, 2016, https://intheblack.com/articles/2016/11/01/top-global-challenges-facing-accounting-practices-today

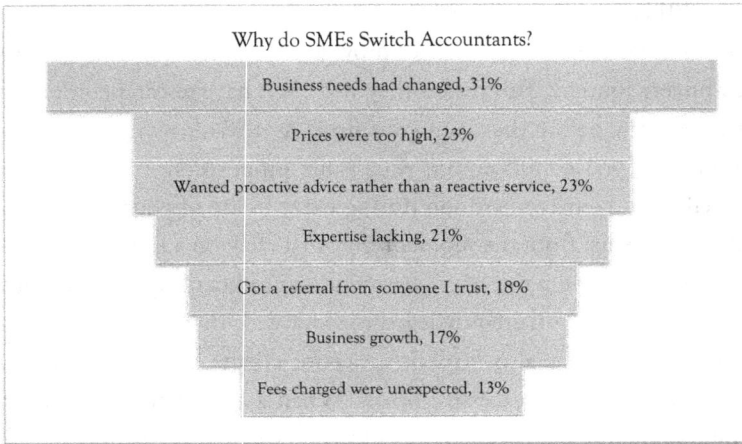

Figure I.1 Key Insights Into the Australian Accounting Industry

The results—Key Insights Into the Australian Accounting Industry—were published in 2018 (see Figure I.1).[5] The report provides some challenging insights into the reasons why businesses change their accountants:

- 31 percent said their business needs had changed.
- 23 percent switched because the prices were too high.
- 23 percent wanted proactive advice rather than a reactive service.

The report also clearly shows that 84 percent of small businesses would prefer their accountant to charge either a fixed or value-based rate (see Figure I.2). Only 16 percent opted for time-based billing. Now if you compare these statistics to the IBIS reports for the accounting industry globally, you will discover there is a massive disconnect between what your clients want and what many of you are prepared to deliver.[6] Roughly 85 percent of the revenue earned by accounting firms still comes from

---

[5] NAB Professional Services. 2018. *Key Insights into the Australian Accounting Industry*, NAB, 2018, https://business.nab.com.au/wp-content/uploads/2018/02/J002905-Professional-Services-Insights-Report_v5.pdf

[6] NAB Professional Services, *Key Insights into the Australian Accounting Industry*.

84% of small businesses prefer to be charged either a
fixed rate or value-based rate.

Fixed fee	54%
Value billing	14%
Client retainer	8%
Per tax form or service	7%
Other	1%
Hourly rate	16%

Only 16% opted for
time-based billing

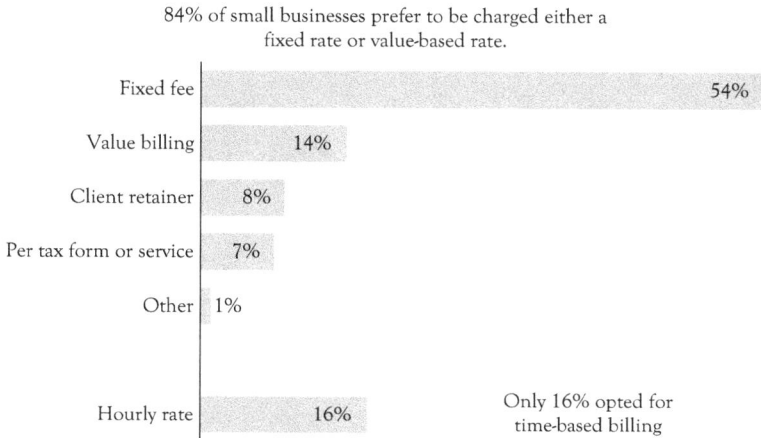

Figure I.2 Client Preference re: Pricing Methodologies

cost-based pricing and compliance work. So it seems that when it comes
to the issue of value and pricing, many accountants are still doing the
exact opposite of what clients actually want.

What Is Pricing Strategy?

When it comes to Pricing Value, there is a lot more to consider than just
what the total price for each client will be. In fact, this book will challenge
you to rethink your overall strategy, your understanding of what consti-
tutes value, your pricing methodologies, tactics and billing methods, and
how to systemize your approach to achieve consistent results.

Your pricing strategy is the overarching way that you approach the
problem of pricing. In most cases, this will mean pricing based on cost
(or a formula derived from your costs) or market forces. Your pricing
methodology, however, is the manner in which you are going to execute
or implement your pricing strategy. For many of you, that will currently
be a combination of hourly and fixed rates (both of which fall into the
category of cost-based pricing) (see Figure I.3).

This diagram gives you a clear visual overview of the two primary pricing strategies and the various methodologies derived from each of those
strategies. This is by no means an exhaustive list and is for illustrative
purposes only.

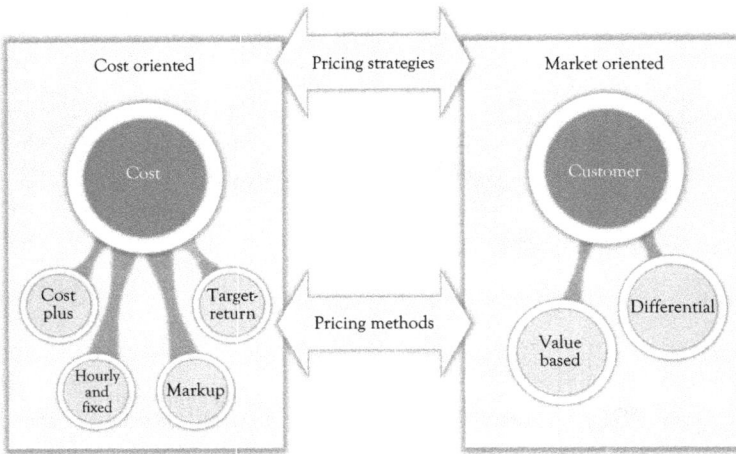

Figure I.3 Pricing Strategies and The Methodologies Associated With Them

More specifically, this book was written to help you examine:

• The pricing strategy your firm will choose to adopt, whether cost or market based.
• Pricing Value (which falls under the umbrella of customer-driven methodologies).
• The distinct point in the engagement process when you will commence the conversation about price.
• How to comprehend, create, capture, and communicate the value of your firm's services to maximize the amount each client is willing to pay.
• How to deflect the attention away from price and expertly manage the factors that directly impact on your client's perception of price.
• How to parcel solutions together (including why and when you should do it).
• The role your payment terms (upfront, monthly recurring, in arrears) play in maximizing your cash flow and the ultimate value of your practice.

The bulk of this book will focus on the specific methodology of Pricing Value because it achieves the perfect balance of certainty, choice, and cure for your client (more about that later and why it is so imperative) and it is backed by scientific, psychological, and systems-based research. Throughout, Pricing Value will be compared and contrasted to hourly rates and fixed packages, so you can easily choose what is best for your practice and your clients.

When value-based pricing is executed correctly—that is, the emphasis and focus are clearly placed on what is of value to the client and delivering that value—then both you and your client are happy and reap the benefits. In fact, when it is implemented masterfully, you are essentially "pricing the value" you bring to the engagement. You charge them the maximum price they are willing to pay based on the value that you deliver. You also reap a higher amount than if you had billed based on time or cost plus margin alone, and the client is happy because the price paid is overshadowed by the value you have helped create.

Unfortunately, the reality is that it is often very challenging for accountants to figure out:

- What is of value to each client?
- How to quantify the value?
- What is the maximum price each client is willing to pay? and
- How to communicate value in a way that is easy for the client to grasp quickly and say "yes" to?

This is especially true for compliance-type services. And to that end, you may have noticed that a number of pricing and proposal software packages have recently appeared—with a few even claiming to help you "value price" your services. Now often these are great proposal tools and they can help you to fix and increase the price you can charge for your compliance work. However, they are not "value-based pricing tools" in the strictest sense of the phrase.

These apps can only help you to set a price (or range of prices) for each of the services that you have to offer, at a rate that is likely to cover your costs and provide a better margin. Unfortunately, as you are about to discover, increased margins will not necessarily boost your cash flow or make your practice more successful and valuable. This controversial and revolutionary topic will be explored in more depth in Chapter 6 because it is in fact integral to the reason why Pricing Value is the only sane option for your accounting firm.

These apps do not have the power to make the current list of services that you have to deliver more valuable to each client and they cannot help you overcome price objections or competition.

Many of these app vendors claim to "start with the client and value in mind." While this sounds positive in theory, what you will find in practice is that most only pay lip service to this very noble intention. If you look closely, you will notice that they are just fixed pricing tools which means they commence with a list of the services you can provide and work backward from there based on your cost structure to arrive at various pricing options. Unfortunately, what your client values is never actually taken into account.

It is in fact impossible to price compliance (or advisory) services in a way that captures the value you bring to the table by using only a spreadsheet, app, or mathematical formula. Anyone who tells you otherwise, does not understand the concept of Pricing Value (or value-based pricing).

Compliance work is often viewed as a "commodity," which essentially is a lazy or crude way of saying that your client sees you as interchangeable in providing it with your competitors. However, if there is a value component (and as you are about to discover, there is always a value component) and it can be elicited, quantified, and acknowledged, then it definitely is possible to transform the engagement into something that can be priced based on value. However, the value component will often be highly subjective, driven by instinctual and survival-based cues, and easily influenced by perceptions and intangible forces. Contrary to popular belief, offering three price options for a service is NOT value-based pricing. What enables you to move into the realm of Pricing Value is your mastery of eliciting value and being able to translate that into a bespoke solution that is no longer viewed as indistinguishable from your competitor's offering.

None of these pricing apps have the capacity to estimate or calculate the value that each individual client attributes to various bespoke solutions to pain points or transformations the client needs to achieve. They merely price each service based on the rules you have input for how much it costs you to deliver management reporting, tax returns, payroll, bank reconciliations, etc., based on certain parameters. Each client is only priced individually to the extent they are paying for a very specific number of services. These apps cannot possibly anticipate or measure what the value of each of those services (or solutions) is in the eyes of your client because each client will attribute value differently.

In actual fact, the only app that can effectively Price Value is the one that sits between your right and left ears. And to engage it and maximize its potential, there is still a bit of work to do in order to ensure you are armed with the right systems, skills, and mindset to get to the heart of "value" first. If you can master the art of identifying and quantifying value before you blindly attempt to offer pricing options you have derived using an app or formula, you will be much more likely to approach the maximum price they are prepared to pay for each engagement.

And finally, it should be noted out that there is no such thing as a "commodity" in business. Well at least not in the strictest sense of the word. Anything can be differentiated or made special: The potential for differentiation is limited only by your imagination and innovation. One of the most destructive beliefs that are held by a large percentage of your colleagues is that tax returns, bookkeeping, payroll, etc., are just commodities. This seemingly innocent but deadly notion is what has produced widespread fear, lack of self-worth, immobilization, the need to copy what others have done versus create, and constant price wars. The time has come for some critical thinking and a fresh perspective, and the future of the profession is riding on it.

Most mistakenly assume technology/apps to be the single biggest factor shaping what it means to be an accountant in this modern era but that view incorrectly puts you outside of the driver's seat. The truth is your pricing methodology is the fulcrum—the point at which you apply pressure to gain significant leverage and impact in your practice. Your tools of the trade (the technology) give you information and opportunity but your pricing plays the central and pivotal role in how you show up in the engagement with your client.

And as you are about to discover...how you show up, means everything.

As You Read This Book...

You may find that the concept of Pricing Value is very foreign or perhaps even a bit scary. You may find yourself thinking "That won't work in my firm" or "We tried that once before, and it failed miserably." If you find yourself struggling to suspend skepticism or maintain a growth mindset, remember, you do have a choice.

You are not obliged to Price Value.

You are free to do what you have always done but remember that choice comes with significant consequences. Your clients will continue to be price conscious and they will also be reluctant to approach you for help with the stuff that's really important to them. And you will continue to resent the fact that you are getting paid far less than the value you bring to the table, and that you make less every year because technology is better than you are at repetitive tasks, classification, anomaly detection, ranking, recommendations, and forecasting (linear regression).

Meanwhile, your competitors will be grappling with the same pivotal question around pricing—especially those Baby Boomers who would like to retire and sell their firms. Some may decide to Price Value, and those that succeed will grow exponentially. You will be required to compete for market share against those firms who are making a significant impact with their clients.

Pricing Value is an art form and the underlying variables that influence success—tangible and perceived value—are changing as your clients' needs and access to other alternatives change. Pricing strategies and methodologies that worked even five years ago may no longer be relevant or could potentially destroy your practice. The future of your firm comes down to how much discomfort you can bear while keeping an open mind and adapting to changing circumstances.

This book was designed to challenge your thinking about the strategies, skills, and mindset you use to price each client. In many cases, the content and the prescription for change will be confronting and contentious. However, no apologies will be made for the fact that sacred cows will indeed be slain in this book.

The real challenge for you is not in accessing more information or insights on pricing, but rather in discerning what to believe and how to implement and test this stuff in your own firm—so you can ask better questions, make better decisions, achieve better results, and step up as the leader of your practice.

Who Is This Book For?

The book is ideal for partners and owners of small to medium-sized accounting firms, who want to ethically and consistently maximize the value of their firm and deepen the relationship (and impact) they have with their small business clients.

If this is you, you are about to discover:

- How to position, price, and package your unique solutions to render price a non-issue.
- How/why your clients buy your services and how it influences the way you market, sell, deliver, and price them.
- How to deal with self-worth issues and eliminate price-sensitive clients.
- How to maximize the value of your firm.
- How to reduce your WIP to almost zero.
- How to influence your clients to SEE the value of your solutions and ask for more.
- How to implement a price increase with little or no resistance.
- How to educate your clients to look forward to quarterly discussions about value and price.
- How to control your own fears and easily make the shift to Pricing Value.
- How to unlearn the bad habits and mindsets that have kept you trapped where you are.

How to Use This Book

You may be tempted to skip the first nine chapters, and go straight to the implementation section. That would be a mistake.

Pricing Value is built on strong foundations—neuroscience, psychology, and systems. Without a strong foundation and thorough understanding of the Pricing Value system, you will essentially be trying to build your practice on the shifting sands. A wise accountant on the other hand, builds his or her firm upon a rock. When the rain, the floods, and the winds of disruption come to beat down your firm, it will stand the test of time and flourish because it is built on solid rock.

Think of the first nine chapters as laying a strong foundation and steel frame in your firm. In order to Price Value proficiently, you must first comprehend the context and foundational skills behind all of the strategies, science, systems, and recommendations.

Pricing Value focuses you on what you need to do in order to uncover and quantify the pain points, dreams, and perceptions that will render price a non-issue and leave your proposed solution as the only sane option. Therefore, in order to Price Value, you need to master the art of correctly eliciting and quantifying those pain points (and desired transformations) so that you can effectively deflect the spotlight away from the price. To achieve this, you will learn a simple step-by-step process that is reliable and robust. Each of the skills is introduced in a specific order to help you to build competence and confidence as you progress through this book.

This book is also supported by a detailed workbook—it contains a series of exercises, templates, and guidelines that have been fully road tested with practices just like yours. It will help you put into practice all that you have learned and give you some tangible systems and structures around Pricing Value so that you can scale the process easily and produce consistent, predictable results.

To kick-start your Pricing Value journey and transform how you show up in your engagements with your clients, pick up the workbook at: pricingvalue.co/workbook

PART I

Mastering the Art of Pricing Value

In order to implement Pricing Value, you must follow a six step process (see Figure P1.1). This graphic is a high level visual overview of what you will learn in this book to help you re-value all of your clients. Part I will deal with the first nine chapters and Part II will cover Chapters 10–14.

First, you will discover and examine the concepts of value and leverage—both require you to have a much deeper understanding of the way the human brain receives, processes, and acts upon data that is received via the five senses. Next, you will be introduced to the six Cs to Pricing Value and how each of those concepts will play an integral role in your journey. The six Cs are:

- Control Your Fear
- Comprehend Value

Pricing Value

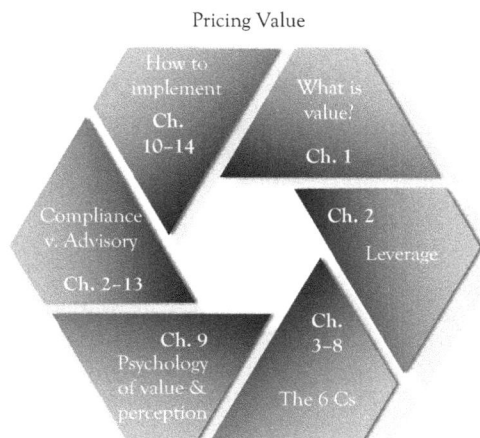

Figure P1.1 Pricing Value Framework – Chapter by Chapter

- Create Value
- Capture Value
- Communicate Value
- Convince

And finally, you will gain a strong appreciation for the domineering role that psychology and neuroscience play in both value and perceived value (as viewed from the eyes of your client). Along the way, the subtle differences between Pricing Value for compliance and advisory will be explored as practical examples and tips of "how to implement" are outlined.

CHAPTER 1

What Is Value?

The question "what is value" has been debated for hundreds of years in the realm of philosophy. One perspective is that value is intrinsic or objective—meaning the value is imposed by some higher power or created by the labor that goes into making a product/service. The other diametrically opposed view is that it is entirely subjective—meaning it's whatever the person wants it to be.

But in truth, you cannot solve the puzzle "what is value" without first answering the questions *to whom* and *for what*. And this is where economics comes in.

The objective theory of value morphed into a labor theory of value as explained at length by Karl Marx in his work, *Das Kapital*.[1] However, this line of thinking led to a classic value paradox, often referred to as the diamond-water paradox, and a lot of unanswered questions.

Here is a quick example of why the diamond-water paradox seriously challenged this old way of thinking. If the amount of labor that went into a good is the sole determinant of its value, a man out on a hike could just as easily stumble upon a diamond or a river and both would therefore, have the same objective value. In this example, both discoveries would require the same amount of labor, yet the diamond would still in most instances be valued much more than the water.

As a result of this paradox, the subjective theory of value was effectively born. Carl Menger was one of the first economists to apply the approach that value is subjectively determined by the individual. As such, value begins in the mind, not with the labor needed to produce a good or service. What this means is your clients have choice—they exercise

---

[1] Karl Marx. Capital, Vol. I, Chapter One, part. I.I.14 "Commodities." Originally published 1867 as Das Kapital.

that choice (whether consciously or unconsciously) to determine which service/solution by which accountant (or other provider) will satisfy their highest ranked need or desired outcome.

So now that you know it is your client who determines value, let's examine what and whom they value.

Is What You Offer Valued by Your Client?

As accounting professionals most of you like to think that you help your clients improve their businesses and cure cash flow problems. The problem is, the vast majority of owners think more customers and sales will cure their cash flow problems and fix their business.

Now, as financial experts, you know that this is not technically correct. More customers does not necessarily lead to improved cash flow. But let's look at another aspect of the problem...

If your clients perceive they need assistance to attract more leads and convert them to fix or grow their business, chances are most will not turn to you first for advice because they currently view you as unqualified in the realm of sales, marketing, pricing, and so on. And to be fair, that observation is technically astute. You need only take a look at your website (or any one of your marketing brochures) to discover that 99 percent of what you say relates to your brand, your experience and credentials, and a laundry list of the services that you provide. Very little time has been invested by you to address what is of value to your ideal client.

Right now clients come to you for a number of reasons—because they need help with bookkeeping, they need a tax return or set of year end accounts completed, or they have questions about payroll and sales tax obligations. And as a professional you have done very well to establish credibility and trust in the realm of "financial expert." But as you've discovered, these tasks are highly price sensitive, limited in scope, and impossible to leverage to create influence with your client.

You've pigeonholed yourself in the box of "financial expert" and now you are stuck there unless you deliberately take action to bust out. And this dilemma is corroborated by a recent study by East & Partners published

Who is your most trusted business adviser?

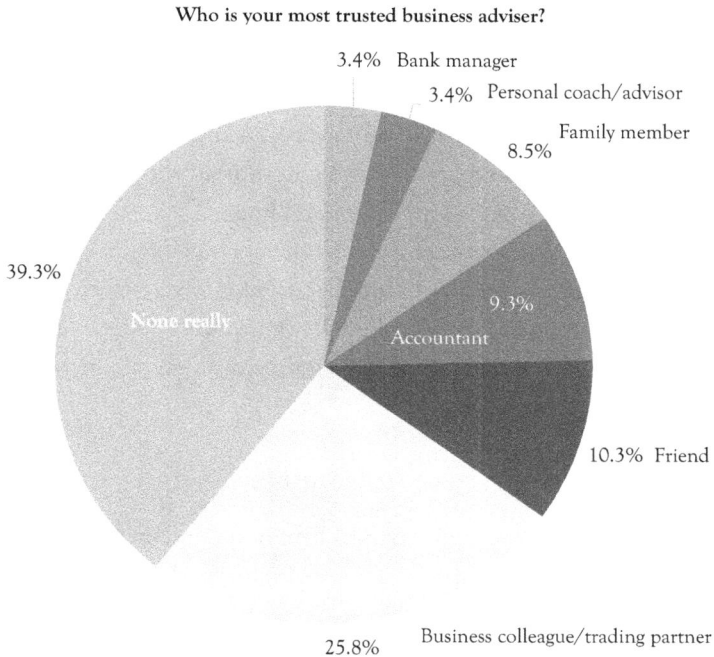

Figure 1.1 Who Small Business Owners Turn To For Advice

in the *Financial Review*.[2] According to that research, only 9.3 percent of small businesses regard their accountant as their most trusted advisor (see Figure 1.1). Yes, you read that correctly, 9.3 percent.

It's an indictment on where our profession stands in the eyes of our clients.

The overwhelming majority (75.4 percent) trust no one, a business colleague, or a friend. And since roughly 85 percent of small business owners are financially illiterate, you can safely conclude that their colleague or friend knows about as much as they do about financials and

---

[2] Who Is Your Most Trusted Business Advisor? East and Partners Survey. 2017. "In Edmund Tadros, Majority of Small Business Owners Don't See Accountants, Lawyers as Trusted Advisors." *Financial Review*, April 4, 2017, https://afr.com/business/accounting/majority-of-small-business-owners-dont-see-accountants-lawyers-as-trusted-advisers-20170403-gvccey

business improvement, which isn't a hell of a lot. Now the good news is that this proves there is enormous potential for you to step up and redefine your role and impact with your small business clients. The only tricky bit is for you to figure out what your client actually values (i.e., what are they willing to pay you for) and how to arm yourself with the right skills, tools, and mindset to deliver that value and impact.

Most of your colleagues are not going to successfully make the transition because they are content (and it feels safe) to stay where they feel comfortable…in the numbers. Thankfully, you already have the edge over those who still have their heads in the sand because you are here with an open mind and ready to learn.

Where to from Here?

Unfortunately, there are two major problems in the accounting industry: a massive skills deficit (in terms of adding real value) and an image problem.

Despite all the talk about moving to advisory and value-based pricing, the truth is most of you have not yet done it. A recent survey[3] highlighted that even in 2016/17, 90 percent of accountants have not yet begun to shift toward advisory services in any meaningful way. In addition, revenue from business advisory services is not growing rapidly and you are being asked to deliver more value each year in compliance with revenue remaining flat or decreasing.

As most of you have discovered, it's not as easy as adding to your website and proposal documents "I'm now providing business advisory" or "I've got some value-priced packages." And the reason for that is simple yet profound—your clients are only willing to pay the big bucks for solutions that are of value to them. And value has been somewhat elusive because until now, you've been looking for it in all the wrong places.

Where Do You Find Value?

The natural inclination for most who embark on the journey is to dedicate 90 percent of their time and attention on the semantics of pricing.

---

[3] Good Bad and Ugly. 2016 and 2017. "Benchmarking Report and Practice Improvement Guide." *Business Fitness,* http://gbuhq.com/download

After all, you are an accountant, so it seems logical to focus on the price because the price is expressed as a number, and you are very good with numbers. The point you have missed is eloquently summed up by Ron Baker, the author of seven best-selling books, several of which focus on pricing—"Pricing is not a number, it's a feeling."

Unfortunately, this preoccupation with pricing semantics has caused you to waste time on factors that only matter to you and the esoteric exercise of determining "the price you need to get" in order to earn a decent living. And that mistake is not entirely your fault because it was driven by factors that are below the level of consciousness and therefore, have gone unnoticed by you until now.

As explained earlier, the phrase "value pricing" is a red herring—value is seen as a mere qualifier to the word "pricing." You've been predisposed from the outset to focus almost all of your attention on the pricing component, and if you think about it, many books, articles, and training programs on the topic follow this pattern. They are marketed with attention grabbing titles such as:

- How to Get the Price You Deserve.
- How to Double Your Price and Avoid Resistance.
- Seven Pricing Strategies of the Most Profitable Firms.
- Eight Steps to Getting a Better Price.
- Using Psychology to Boost Your Prices.

But here's the problem…

The most important word in the phrase Pricing Value is of course "value." And value, while determined by your client, must be masterfully uncovered and drawn out by you, the practitioner. Value may not be something your client can easily articulate or quantify without your expert assistance. In fact, some of the most valuable information and insights may be pain points, experiences or transformations, and feelings that even your clients themselves are not yet fully aware of.

One of the reasons why it is so vital to completely turn the concept of value pricing inside out (or back to front) is because of the imperative for you to focus the bulk of your time, energy, and resources on the fundamental driver—VALUE. And to do that, we must first place the word value where it rightfully deserves to be positioned, as the focal point and key ingredient of the phrase.

Thus, the new call to action—Pricing Value.

When you shift to Pricing Value, your #1 job is crystal clear. Your most pressing concern is patently obvious—you need to ascertain what is of value to your clients. And then off the back of that—why it is of value, how valuable it is, and what you need to do in order to help them achieve it.

In a nutshell, Pricing Value is the process you must employ in order to uncover and quantify the pain points, transformations, feelings, and perceptions that will cause price to become a non-issue in the eyes of your clients, thus rendering your proposed solution the only sane option. Pricing Value focuses both you and your client squarely on what is of value to them and their priorities to fix issues or achieve results. And it deflects the spotlight away from the price. In fact, it's the only way to avoid "sticker shock" and the constant threat of price objections.

In order to effectively Price Value (i.e., price the value that you bring to the table, rather than trying to make the price you want to offer seem more valuable), you must follow a six step process (refer back to Figure P1.1). This graphic provides a high level visual overview of what is important when shifting your clients (new and existing) over to a pricing model that reflects the true value of the engagement.

How Do You Determine What Is of Value?

In order to explore this crucial question and help you take the insights in at a much deeper level, let's look at an example using a simple product that you probably think you have a good handle on the value of.

Let's assume for a moment that someone has placed a simple glass of water on the table or the desk in front of you right now as you are reading this book. Just so you know, the water was filtered and chilled so you can expect it to be cold and refreshing. But as you well know, even though water is a thirst-quenching beverage, it's often viewed as not being worth much.

Right now, sitting where you are sitting in the comfort of your chair, presumably with easy access to the tap in your own office or home, how much is this glass of water really worth? If you would pay more than a couple of cents for it, that would be most unusual.

Can you actually imagine paying more than a couple of cents for it right now? Of course not. Why would you? You can get up from your chair, walk to your sink or water cooler, and pour a refreshing glass for yourself, free of charge.

Now what if the person who placed that glass of water on your table or desk used some old-school sales and marketing techniques on you? The pitch to get you to part with your hard earned money to buy the glass of water at a premium price might sound something like this… "This water was drawn from a million year old glacier in Canada by virgin hands and stored in a solid gold vessel before it was flown on the wings of doves to your doorstep. In fact, it's an award winning glass of water and here is a list of all the amazing benefits and things that you can do with it…"

Apologies for the overly dramatic spiel, but hopefully you can recognize the ridiculous yet only-too-familiar tactics at play.

In fact, in your lifetime you've probably listened politely to thousands of advertisements exactly like this even though deep down you knew you had no intention of buying X for a premium price. And at the end of each pitch, you probably produced an excuse very similar to "the glass of water is just too expensive" or "I need more time to think about it."

Unfortunately, 99 percent of the messages that you've been using to sell your accounting services are exactly like this. You have a powerful solution that can help your clients to fix and transform their businesses, but you are making the rookie mistake of diluting your message with your accounting service.

Let's examine what this means by referring back to the earlier example…

First ask yourself, "If the glass of water were your accounting service, what would your message need to be in order to sell it for a premium price?"

It's a fascinating question, isn't it?

Does it make sense, knowing how plentiful and cheap water (and your accounting service) is, to focus on features and benefits, emphasize your brand, or list all your accounting services, awards, or certifications?

Is an advertisement full of stuff about YOU, the services you provide, and your qualifications really going to help you command a premium price?

The answer to that question is of course, NO. But if you are being honest, isn't that exactly what you have been doing?

If you are not sure, put down this book and pull up your firm's website (or your last proposal) on your computer. How much of what you see is about you and what you can do? Is any of it specifically about your ideal client and the stuff that is keeping him/her up at night?

When you feel the need to talk about your accounting services, the fact you are a trusted advisor, or your value-based packages, instead of focusing on your client's key pain points, feelings, or desired transformations and what he or she needs to do to fix them, you are essentially "diluting your message and impact." Many of the compliance tasks that your client has come to you for help with are in fact very similar to the glass of water in this example. There are hundreds of thousands of qualified professionals who can also do those tasks and 90 percent have made no attempt to differentiate or make the work special/unique. Like the glass of water, undifferentiated accounting services are plentiful and cheap and that is why you are stuck competing based on price.

Those compliance tasks are not the important things that are keeping your clients awake at night, losing sleep. The pain points, feelings they have, and the desired transformation they need to achieve, is what has sparked a deep thirst and hunger within them—but they are still unsure where to find the solution.

When a small business client comes to you because they are thirsty for the knowledge and business improvement solutions you have—shouldn't you ask:

- Why are you thirsty (i.e., what is keeping you up at night)?
- How thirsty are you (i.e., how much does this problem cost you)?
- What would a solution to X be worth to you right now?

The shift to Pricing Value is a potent and purposeful one. It focuses you squarely on building up the depth of your client's thirst instead of focusing on why your water (i.e., accounting service) is better than your competition.

And this is a really crucial point, which 99 percent of accountants will completely miss.

To Price Value, you need to find out:

- Why your clients are in pain, how they feel about it, and/or what desired transformation(s) they need to achieve?
- What the magnitude of that pain is or the disparity between where they are now and where they want to be?
- What you need to do to provide the solution?

It doesn't make sense to focus on you, your brand, your services, or even your value-based packages. All of these are a distraction from your main purpose of understanding the depth of the pain (or the magnitude of the experience or transformation they want to achieve), providing the solution, and proving that you can deliver it.

And if you are still not convinced, let's come back to the glass of water we discussed earlier.

Only a moment ago you were asked to consider how much you were prepared to pay for that glass of water—and you agreed, at the time, not very much.

But what if you were on an eight-hour road trip with two thirsty, screaming toddlers and the only place you could find water was in a bottle at 7/11. Would you be willing to pay a bit more in order to get some peace in the car and stop the tantrums? For those of you who are parents and can relate to this example, $6 probably seems like a bargain to you right now, doesn't it?

How about if you were on a holiday with your family in a third world country and you couldn't drink out of the tap because it was contaminated? Would you be willing to pay a bit more again for some clean bottled water from the hotel gift shop? $10 doesn't seem so bad when the health of your family is at risk, does it?

And what if you were stranded in the desert without a drink for 48 hours, in 104° F (40°C) heat, and you'd been crawling across the sand trying to find someone to rescue you? Would you be prepared to pay $100 or even $1,000 for that same, simple glass of cool, filtered water?

In fact, if you think about it, isn't your life worth at least that much, if not more?

Here's the thing… The value of the water (or your accounting service) is directly related to the amount of pain that your client is in right now. If the pain is excruciating (or it is a matter of life of death), your client will pay any price to acquire the solution, but they will only pay pennies for your features and benefits, your brand, your undifferentiated accounting services, or your awards and accreditations.

This is the essence of what VALUE truly is and it's why you must always Price Value and not get led down the garden path of focusing way too much time, energy, and resources on the semantics of pricing.

This crucial point leads directly to the next step in the Pricing Value module that you must master—Leverage.

In order to gain leverage, you must to do your homework up front and learn the right questions to ask. Questions are in fact the answers. With better questions, you will gain better insight into what is of value to each client.

Contrary to what you previously thought the hurdles were to making the shift to value-based pricing, the truth is it all comes down to VALUE and LEVERAGE. You need to strip away all the noise and clutter that's diluting your message and effectiveness, and preventing you from comprehending value and establishing leverage. To Price Value, you must focus squarely on the #1 thing that's driving your client's thirst (their pain points, feelings, and desired transformations), what you need to do to solve it, and what you need to say to help them say "YES" to working with you.

And most importantly, if you want to step into the role of advisor or to offer packages that capture the value and impact you bring to the table, it is incumbent upon you to invest in yourself to learn the right skills, tools, and mindset. If you are not willing to invest in yourself to bridge the skills deficit or redefine what your role is with your clients, then what right do you have to ask them to invest in you as their advisor?

Until you change, you will struggle to find and retain higher paying clients.

CHAPTER 2

The Power of Leverage

Roughly 85 percent[1] of the small business clients that you work with are financially illiterate—and that statistic is likely conservative. These clients are easy to spot because they consistently struggle to pay the bills as they fall due, or pay themselves a decent wage. These are also the same clients who don't pay your invoices on time and expect you to work for peanuts because they don't value what you do behind the scenes to help keep them afloat.

Kerry, an accountant and bookkeeper, found herself exactly in your shoes with a tradesman client that she had been working with for about three years. On the one hand, she saw enormous potential in his business because he was very good at what he did, but on the other, she worried that he was expanding too quickly and making poor decisions. He simply did not fully grasp the implications of pricing, hiring, and credit choices on his profit and cash flow.

Kerry was in an unenviable position. She knew that she could help him to ask better questions, make better decisions, and ultimately get better results, but first, she had to get him to agree to accept help and take action to do the work she suggested. Because he was constantly in a cash crunch, he felt he simply couldn't afford her existing services—the payroll runs, bank reconciliations, and sales tax returns—let alone the work she was proposing to do with him as a value-priced engagement.

She tried several times to get him to look at her new "value-priced packages" but he always gave her the same response: "It's more than I can afford right now and I need time to think about it." As you can imagine, Kerry felt pretty frustrated and she was beginning to think that

---

[1] Data and statistics provided by Australian Treasury Department—Key Statistics and Analysis December 2012.

value-based pricing, while it sounded great in theory, was just not going to work with price conscious clients like her tradesman.

And if you think about it, this is probably exactly where you find yourself right now. Because of the nature of the work you do for your clients and your past experience (which has taught you that price is often an issue), you anticipate the move to Pricing Value will be somewhat challenging.

But here's the thing… With one small shift in your mindset around "what is of value," and a simple yet powerful tool called Leverage, moving all your clients to Pricing Value packages is about to become much easier than you first imagined.

Why Do Clients Resist Your Increases?

Believe it or not, your client's price objections and requests for more time to think about it are a huge blessing in disguise.

When he or she says "I need to think about it" or "I can't afford it, it's just too expensive," what they are essentially telling you is that you've made a simple (but correctable) error by triggering the wrong parts of your client's brain with your message. Getting this sort of feedback from your client is actually very valuable and helpful. It means that with some simple, yet profound changes to how you approach and communicate with your clients, you can make it much easier for them to say "yes."

Thanks to neuroscience, we now have a lot more clarity and insight about how the brain receives, processes, and acts upon the stimuli you take in from each of your five senses—sight, touch, taste, hearing, and smell.

And this brain research corroborates what experts like Michael LeBoeuf, Joseph Pine, and James Gilmore have been saying for decades—people buy *emotionally* (or based on instinct and survival) and justify their decision *intellectually*. In a nutshell, what this means is that your clients are not interested in your accounting services. Rather, your future lies in your ability to identify and give them what they do want and are willing to pay top dollar for. And this comes down to two very straightforward things:

- solutions to pain points
- transformation, experiences, and feeling good/safe

Since clients buy solutions, transformation, and experiences that feel good/safe, then it's your job to figure out how to provide them. This means that it's incumbent upon you to delve deep and understand the feelings, desire for change, and pain points your clients have and also how they go about processing information to make a decision to buy from you. Let's examine how neuroscience has an impact on how you and your clients create, buy, sell, and experience everything.

If your client is worried about price or "needs to think about it," it is highly likely that your message is being assessed and processed by the neo cortex and prefrontal cortex (collectively known as the cerebral cortex). While the brain is a whole system and all aspects and circuits are engaged and collaborating with each other at all times, the cerebral cortex lights up when processing words, numbers, colors, making spatial comparisons, or looking for data. In a nutshell, this part of the brain is primarily associated with thinking, and when your brain does so, it uses up tons of energy—which prolongs the decision-making process.[2]

While thinking may not seem like a big deal, your brain demands a significant amount of power to fuel this activity. Your brain contains 1 million kilometers of interconnected fiber and over 100 billion neurons, and they all require energy. While your brain only weighs a few kilograms, it consumes 25 percent of your body's total energy. Because of this extraordinary consumption, power conservation is crucial to your survival. That is why your brain is hardwired to conserve energy when and where it can. One of the ways it does this is to rest (wherever possible) and also expedite decision making by relying on automatic mechanisms to make decisions or take action.[3]

So, by all means, if you want to drag out the process of getting your clients to decide, you definitely want to make sure they do as much thinking as possible which is very taxing on the brain. Give your clients lots of words, numbers, graphs, features, and benefits, and list all of your awards

---

[2] Zurawicki, L. 2010. *Neuromarketing: Exploring the Brain of the Consumer*, 77–85. London & New York, NY: Springer Heidelberg Dordrecht.
[3] Korolak, R. 2012. *Sales Seduction: Why Do You Say Yes?* 4. Melbourne: Imagineering Now Pty. Ltd.

and accreditations—and your clients will NOT decide but they will do a whole lot of thinking and waste your time in the process.

So it begs the question, "If humans are hardwired to make decisions using as little energy as possible, how [exactly] does your brain decide and act?"

There are several brain structures that support basic survival functions, complex automatic behavior, adaptive behavior sequence optimization, and emotions. These include but are not limited to your brainstem and hypothalamus, the limbic system (including your temporal lobe, hippocampus, and the amygdala), and basal ganglia. Many years ago, behavioral psychologists and other researchers began referring to these collectively as the "old (or reptilian) brain". The catchy "old brain" label has endured even though modern neuroscience has proven the brain did not evolve in layers and that the Triune (new, middle, and reptilian) brain model is in fact overly simplistic and inaccurate.

What this means is that at a broad conceptual level, the brain is a whole, interdependent system. However, in moments of fight-or-flight, the automatic systems take over to expedite decision making and conserve energy. All bodily functions that take place below the level of consciousness emanate from these automated structures in your brain. That is why so many refer to it collectively as your "fight-or-flight brain" because it's directly responsible for ensuring your survival.

As a result, survival-related functions and emotions dominate your decision-making process because these automated structures exert a strong influence on the other parts of your brain. Unlike your cerebral cortex, these fight-or-flight structures are automatic mechanisms. They do not have the same capacity to think and reason. They light up when you decide and act.[4] In fact, these structures within the brain light up long before you have conscious awareness that you have even made a decision. Research suggests they "see" things in 1–2 milliseconds, whereas it takes 500 milliseconds for those same visual cues to reach the cerebral cortex.

---

[4] Dr. Maltz, M. 1960. *Psycho-Cybernetics*. California: Psycho-Cybernetics Foundation.

They also process visual images 40 times faster than auditory cues.[5] These automatic mechanisms are primarily driven by visual cues, emotions, and primitive instincts. Neuroscience has proven that they struggle to process words and numbers.[6]

These parts of your brain are always at work scanning the environment for information of value to your survival. Therefore, in order to help your clients use the least amount of brain energy when processing your new value-based offers and trigger a quick decision in your favor, you must stimulate and appeal to these structures (hereinafter collectively referred to as the "old brain" for illustrative purposes and simplification only).

If the Old Brain Can't Read, How Will You Price Value?

So, you might be sitting there thinking, "How is it even possible to influence and convince these structures within the brain to respond to value-based packages, because pricing is largely based on words and numbers?" If the old brain of your client cannot understand numbers or language, how are you going to help your clients to decide and say "yes"?

Unfortunately, the more complicated the system you use to comprehend, create, capture, and communicate value, the more likely it is that you will put your client to sleep—or worse, overwhelm the decision-making parts of their brain and cause them to have to "think about it."

In order to captivate the attention of and compel the old brain to react positively to your value-based offers and communications, you must first learn to do one thing—speak the language of the old brain.

---

[5] Suied, C., and I. Viaud-Delmon. April 2009. "Auditory-Visual Object Recognition Time Suggests Specific Processing for Animal Sounds." *PLoS One* 4, no. 4. doi.org/10.1371/journal.pone.0005256

Also, Jain, A., R. Bansal, A. Kumar, and K.D. Singh. 2015. "A Comparative Study of Visual and Auditory Reaction Times on the Basis of Gender and Physical Activity Levels of Medical First Year Students." *International Journal of Applied and Basic Medical Research* 5, no. 2, p. 124.

[6] Zoccolan, D., D. Cox, and A. Benucci. 2015. "What Can Simple Brains Teach Us About How Vision Works?" *Frontiers in Neural Circuits* 9, p. 51.

All of the tips, templates, and tactics contained in typical value-pricing courses are of no use to you unless you first learn to speak the language of the true decision-maker—the old brain. By learning to speak the language of the old brain, you gain the most important ingredient to building a successful and thriving accounting practice—LEVERAGE.

Mastering leverage makes it possible to Price Value quickly and effectively—because it simplifies your message, reduces the amount of time it takes your clients to decide, and ensures what you say is of value to them. And it will work no matter which medium or channel you choose to communicate it in.

Make no mistake, the language of the old brain is incredibly primitive and restrictive. Thankfully, it is also incredibly simple, easy to remember, and when used correctly, it will produce predictable and reliable results with your ideal clients in every aspect of your practice!

By mastering the systems outlined in this book, you will have everything you need to re-engineer your client's decision-making process. You will be able to go back to the beginning, ask better questions, and revise what you say and how you say it, in order to influence a speedy decision in your favor.

This simple process for gaining leverage has been put together for one reason—to make it easier for your client to see the value of your new proposed solution and how it will help them to solve the pain points that keep them up at night or help them achieve a desired transformation. When you make it easy for your clients to see the value and grasp it with their old brain, they are much more likely to make a decision quickly. They will on some level also appreciate the fact that you have not wasted their time and energy with stuff that is only important to you, not them.

What Is Leverage?

Leverage, as defined by *The Free Dictionary*, is:

- The mechanical advantage gained by employing a lever.
- Power to accomplish something; a strategic advantage.

The final point succinctly sums up the essence of leverage in the context of Pricing Value. It is in fact the "strategic advantage" that delivers the leverage you need to Price Value. And it is the essence of why you can have the same technical list of credentials and services as your competitor, yet wield the power to capture infinitely more revenue because you have deliberately chosen to Price Value.

As you are quickly discovering, focusing on information that means something to you (but not to your client) is of little or no use if you truly want to capture the value of what you bring to the engagement. The "traditional" approaches to weaning your clients off hourly rates and onto packages that are fixed or value-priced have little or no impact on the real decision-maker of your client—the old brain.

An eloquent, comprehensive, and logical message is often not going to be enough to convince them and get them across the line—in order to have maximum impact, the old brain of your client needs to SEE, remember, and feel compelled to ACT. You need leverage to make that impact on the decision-making part of your client's brain.

If your message is relevant, highly visual, memorable, and easy to grasp, and there is sufficient motivation to take action, your client is much more likely to prioritize the need to take action to fix their pain points or achieve the transformation (or experience) they seek.

It is impossible to have influence and Price Value if you do not first have sufficient leverage. Leverage is in fact the key to everything, and it is the factor that 99 percent of your competitors are currently missing or overlooking. If you don't first get leverage, it is impossible to sell and deliver value-based services. Leverage is the secret sauce that makes clients engage and it's what ensures that they focus on value (not price), and take action. And remember, if your clients don't take action, or worse, they expect you to do all of the work for them, you will remain stuck in the perilous pit of cost-plus pricing models.

How Do You Get Leverage?

In order to make an impact and gain strategic advantage, the old brain of your potential client needs to be awake and alert when you deliver your proposed solution. What you say first must create an indelible impression and captivate their undivided attention.

That is why the most important step in Pricing Value—creating an offer that your clients can't refuse—is to become an expert at capturing attention and holding it. If you are successful at enchanting your client within the first 60 seconds, you stand a much greater chance of holding his or her interest (i.e., keeping the old brain awake) long enough to communicate your entire message and proposed pricing packages.

Remember, your client's brain is energy hungry. It is constantly looking for an opportunity to power down and rest. Since it is primarily concerned with your client's physical survival, it will operate at near maximum alertness at the beginning and end of every interaction with you. However, your client's level of attentiveness will drop down to as low as 20 percent in the middle of every dealing he or she has with you.[7]

Once your client's old brain has scanned the environment and determined that it is safe to be with you, it will power down and tune out. That is why your client will be most alert and will pay particular attention to the very first and the last thing that you say or present to them.

So in the context of Pricing Value, here is the key to leverage—in order to capture the attention of your client and hold it throughout your entire interaction with them, you must know the one (or two) thing(s) that is/are MOST important to him or her right now. This is something that you cannot afford to guess or assume. You must know each client's key pain points, feelings, desire for transformation, and motivations intimately, and have a strong idea in the back of your mind what will be required to deliver the solution, BEFORE you present your solution or value-based pricing.

As you can imagine, with thousands of apps and solutions in the ecosystem, it is going to be virtually impossible for you to master the ability to deliver complex, holistic business solutions across every industry.

And this is why the concept of niching down is particularly relevant and powerful in the context of Pricing Value. At the moment, clients come to you from many diverse industries and backgrounds and you are able to successfully do the work (with little input from them) and deliver the invoice based on your time. In order to Price Value, your client must commit upfront to an engagement that is much more open-ended and

---

[7] Blanchette, J.F., and D.G. Johnson. 2002. "Data Retention and the Panoptic Society: The Social Benefits of Forgetfulness." *The Information Society 18*, no. 1, pp. 33–45.

one that includes solutions to key pain points (and/or desired transformations) that they themselves have now prioritized.

Unlike payroll, bank reconciliations, tax returns, and so on, these key pain points, feelings, and desire for transformation are much more complex in nature (with many variables involved) and the path to solving them will be somewhat unclear. In order for you to confidently Price Value, you must master the skills to elicit and quantify each of those pain points, feelings, or need for transformation AND have a solid idea in the back of your mind of what it will take to capture that value in an engagement, plus deliver the solution.

In order to gain leverage and charm the old brain of your client, you need to do your homework up front. By taking the time to help your client see, acknowledge, and quantify pain (or the disparity between where he or she is now and where they would like to be), they will become clear about the true source and intensity of the pain or the transformation they desire, and you will reinforce with their old brain that it is safe to trust you and your proposed value-based solution. That is the essence of leverage.

And if you think about it, this is the exact approach that you would expect and demand from other professionals that you trust with the things that are most important to you—how your doctor assesses your health or the health of your children, your mechanic assesses the roadworthiness of your vehicle, your pilot conducts preflight checks before you take off, and so on.

Would you feel safe if your doctor blindly dispensed medication without first establishing that you don't have pre-existing conditions, allergies, or other prescriptions that might cause a negative reaction? What if your pilot arrived two minutes before take-off, hopped into the cockpit and just took it on blind trust that the fuel, engines, landing gear, and emergency equipment were in good working order?

Identifying Pain or Need for Transformation to Gain Leverage

Before you can hope to seize and captivate your client's undivided attention, you must first discover his or her pain points and get clear about what they need to achieve in order to have the experience or transformation they desire.

Pain can present itself in many different forms—not just stuff related to their numbers. In order to establish whether it is financial, personal, or strategic, you need to find a way to diagnose it accurately and consistently. For most clients, financial pain will be the easiest for you to uncover and measure because it can be easily quantified and you are trained to make these sorts of assessments. Financial pain normally presents itself as poor cash flow, and it is often be measured by a well accepted key performance indicators.

Strategic pain is often more difficult to measure but it is just as significant and usually tied to the way that the organization goes about producing, distributing, and selling their products or services. To uncover strategic pain, you will want to explore business risk, quality issues, productivity, employee turnover, delivery challenges, supplier issues, market positioning, market share, branding, and other similar issues.

Personal pain may reveal itself to you as work/life imbalance, difficulty sleeping, strained relationships, excessive stress, indecisiveness, bad habits, and fear of moving forward. Any challenges that relate to the feelings and emotions that your prospect has around their financial or strategic issues and resolving them will fall under the heading of personal pain. The other way that personal pain can show up is when the client has (or discovers through working with you) a compelling vision or desire for transformation. The need to change or revolutionize some aspect of themselves or the business is very powerful—especially if it is so enthralling and compelling that it drives them to snap out of complacency and take immediate action to achieve it.

You create a solid system that you can use repeatedly in your practice to uncover, comprehend, and quantify pain (including the desire to achieve transformation or avoid bad feelings such as guilt, shame, or anxiety), by asking probative questions such as:

- "What is the biggest challenge you face in your business?"
- "When you think of fixing the problem of X in your business, what is the most difficult issue associated with putting a solution in place?"

This exercise is invaluable when you Price Value for two reasons.

1. You are about to discover the exact nature and magnitude of the pain your clients are in (or the frustration they feel because they do not have the results they want).
2. You will finally grasp that your clients aren't interested in the services or packages that you have to sell. In fact, they are only interested in finding the solution(s) to solve their financial, strategic, and personal pain (including the need to avoid bad feelings or achieve transformation).

And once you comprehend what is of value to them and how deeply it is impacting your client, you will be in the best place to position and price your solution—instead of merely trying to flog your value-priced packages.

It is crucial to remember that your clients aren't interested in your new value-priced packages. In fact, they likely don't even know what the phrase means. They only see value in, and are willing to pay handsomely for, solutions that cure their pain or help them achieve a desired transformation. Once your clients fully grasp and comprehend their specific pain points (or desire to transform their results) and are able to tell you what is giving them the most discomfort or concern, then and only then will you have achieved leverage.

Leverage is the best starting point from which to build your portfolio of valuable, in-demand solutions. In order for these solutions and your messaging around them to be impactful and compelling, you first must do the hard work up front and pinpoint the specific pain or desire for transformation that each client has.

It is also worth noting that all pain is not created equal. Do not waste your valuable time focusing on low intensity concerns. The greater the pain (or the farther they are away from having the feelings or results they desire), the greater the resources that are being employed by your client right now to focus on the problem. This represents a fantastic opportunity (i.e., leverage) for you to redirect all of their wasted time, money, and resources to acquire your solution.

Finally, you will also need to establish whether your client is sufficiently motivated to alleviate the pain or put in the hard yards required to achieve their dream. Urgency and leverage are directly proportionate to the consequence that will be suffered if the pain is not cured (or the transformation is not achieved). Your client is more likely to act if consequences are imminent or costs are mounting each day. If there is not enough urgency and leverage around a particular pain point (or desired transformation), your client will tend to put off making a decision. That's because his or her old brain is hardwired to focus on whatever is most critical to their survival right now.

It is impossible to Price Value in the absence of having a deep and intimate understanding of the pain points, feelings, and desire for transformation. Every day you have opportunities to captivate and influence your clients in your interactions with them. But how many of these valuable opportunities do you waste by trying to teach them accounting, focusing on the services you have to sell, or presenting information that is important to you but not relevant to them?

Shouldn't the very first thing that you say in each interaction with your client recreate or identify the primary pain, feelings, or desire for transformation, that you know he or she has?

How much more effective would your offer be, if your clients knew from the outset that you understood their #1 source of pain (or desire for transformation) and that you have the solution?

Using Value and Leverage to Implement Pricing Value

When you take time up front to help your clients comprehend, acknowledge, and quantify the pain points that are keeping them up at night, you gain leverage. This is because you become crystal clear about the true source and intensity of the pain (or the disparity between where they are and where they need to be), and you reinforce that it is safe to trust you and your proposed solution. Then, and only then, will you be in a position to price your client correctly.

As Kerry discovered in our example earlier when she tried to introduce her value-priced packages before taking time up front to identify and quantify her client's specific pain points, price and timing are the most common objections. She didn't know it then, but she had inadvertently made the rookie mistake of premature quotation. She tried to match her client to the packages that she had derived instead of taking time up front to get leverage by fundamentally comprehending the pain points her client desperately needed solutions for.

Thankfully, she was able to go back, start at the beginning and take her time to gain leverage and establish trust organically. By spending more time up front and getting clear on what was of value to her tradesman client, she was able to establish that growth/expansion were important to him. He wanted to build a solid team around himself so that he could stop working seven days a week and have more time to spend with his young family. Knowing this, and also being able to pinpoint the primary sources of his cash flow pain, made it easy for an experienced practitioner like Kerry (who specializes in working with plumbers and electricians), to create a custom solution for him and price it with the value/impact in mind.

Within a very short period of time, she was able to help him boost his cash flow by 73 percent which meant he got to safely bring on another qualified tradesman. This freed him up to have weekends off and reduce his hours down to eight per day.

And as you can imagine, Kerry's confidence and job satisfaction increased significantly, while she quietly billed an incremental 27 percent each month on her engagement with him.

Remember, in the absence of comprehending value and gaining leverage, you cannot Price Value. Pricing Value is not a number, formula, or three packages that you present—it's an experience and a feeling. The stronger the overall experience and the impact you create, the greater the value your client will attribute to working with you.

Contrary to what you thought the hurdles might be in making the shift to Pricing Value (i.e., the price consciousness of your clients), the truth is that it all comes down to value and leverage. It doesn't make sense to immediately jump into a discussion about what price to charge, how many options you should give clients, whether your prices should end in "9," and so on. The correct approach is to spend 90 percent of your time focusing on value and leverage, and only 10 percent on the semantics of pricing.

Pricing Value forces you to strip away all the noise and clutter that is diluting your message and effectiveness, so you can focus on the #1 thing that's driving your client's thirst (i.e., their pain and/or vision for the future) and what you need to do to solve it—and thus help them to say "yes" to taking action right now.

Here's the thing, if your client walks away today and does not decide, the pain will not fix itself and their desired transformation will not be achieved by divine intervention. Your client's brain is hardwired to keep searching for the solution. Unfortunately, there are plenty of business coaches and consultants out there, far less qualified than you to actually solve the pain (especially if it is financial), but more adept at eliciting value, gaining leverage, and selling their solution. Pricing Value is your opportunity to step up and build the sort of relationships with your clients that you were always destined to have.

CHAPTER 3

C#1 Control Your Fear

In 1990, Alan Hobson and Jamie Clarke were typical 21-year-old Canadian men. Both loved the outdoors, were avid sportsmen, and shared a childhood dream to reach the summit of Mt. Everest. Only problem was, neither one of them had any actual mountaineering experience. But that was just a minor detail…

Due to an opportunistic twist of fate, a Canadian climbing expedition received a sponsorship of $100,000 from Magnavox to take their satellite phone to Everest in order to test and showcase it under the harshest of circumstances. John McIssac, the leader, was quick to snatch up the money, which was desperately needed to fund equipment and logistics, but he quickly realized that they didn't have any technical experts on the team to manage the satellite phone and deliver on their promise to Magnavox.

Enter Hobson and Clarke.

Clarke had been sniffing around the team for years, looking to land a role that would take him closer to his childhood dream. He wasn't about to let a simple thing like "actual experience operating satellite technology" ruin his big chance. With a dash of literary liberty on their resumes, Hobson and Clarke landed roles as technical experts to support the Canadian team at Base Camp and they executed the first live broadcast from Base Camp. And as fate would have it, due to the illness and injuries of other team members, both ended up being part of two failed attempts to the summit in 1991 and 1994.

By 1994, the team, which now included Hobson and Clarke as experienced mountaineers, made a courageous effort to reach the summit without the use of oxygen, only to have to turn back less than 500 feet from the top. McIssac succumbed to fatigue and extreme altitude sickness. Torn between survival and their lifelong dream, the team had no choice but to turn back in order to save his life.

Now here's where the story gets really interesting…

In addition to a treacherous descent in gale force winds, the entire team was now charged with the enormous responsibility of getting McIssac back down to 26,000 feet where the team doctor was on stand-by. Slowly they saw his life slipping away. Not only was he suffering from severe altitude sickness and pulmonary edema, but also he was spent mentally and had lost his will to live. He couldn't walk two steps without collapsing to the ground. Everyone knew the entire team was at risk of dying on that mountain if they could not ignite the spark within McIssac to live.

In desperation, Hobson remembered that McIssac had made his two young daughters a promise that he would not die on Everest, so they fired up the satellite phone. They put the receiver to his ear while he lay motionless on the ice, so that he could hear the voices of his girls. While the grown men, some of the most experienced climbers in the world, were terrified and panicking as they faced certain death straight in the eye, those two little girls were completely calm and unfazed. They urged, "Daddy, don't you forget your promise. We love you and we want you to come home."

And for the first time in 20 minutes, McIssac slowly started to move. He clambered to his feet only to take one step and again fall to the ground, but his girls stayed right there on the line with him and said, "Daddy, we love you. When are you going to be home?" It was as if those two little girls reached across the miles, picked that tired man up, put him back on his feet, and urged him ever so gently to come home to them.

The team took a rope, tied a knot, and tethered themselves to McIssac—inextricably linking their lives and their fates together as they began to slowly coax and lower him down the mountain. And fueled by the love of his daughters and his desire to fulfill his promise, he somehow found the strength to make the grueling six-hour trek back to High Camp, by the end of which he was crawling on his hands and knees.

When asked to quantify on a scale of 1 to 10 (1 being fine and 10 being death) the severity of McIssac's condition, the doctor rated him as 9/10. He administered medication and oxygen treatment and they initiated an emergency evacuation down the mountain to get him to a hospital. Four hours into the descent, McIssac lost consciousness. His vital signs deteriorated significantly and he began to froth at the mouth as the liquid in his lungs started to come out. At that point, they weren't sure if he was even going to make it, but the team pushed forward anyway.

They put McIssac into a sleeping bag and a stretcher with a harness, and began to slowly lower him down the North Face of Everest for hours. Eventually they got him to the safety of a hospital where he received life-saving medical attention and was able to make good on his promise to return safely to his daughters.

Now granted, the challenge you face right now in Pricing Value isn't life threatening for you as a person, but it is in fact vital to the health and survival of your practice. Many of the thoughts, fears, beliefs, excuses, and bad habits that have held you back from charging based on the value you deliver are equally as daunting and debilitating. These fears keep you trapped in a vicious circle of working harder and way longer hours than you should. And along the way, you may have even broken promises to your family, team members, clients, or even yourself, because of them.

But like McIssac, even if the severity of the situation you find yourself in right now in your practice is a 9/10 (near death), there is a way forward. You need to find a way to harness your fear, tie a knot in the rope (i.e., commit) so you can leverage the best strategies that exist to Price Value, and start climbing toward engagements that create more value for you and your clients.

Facing the Fear

On their third and final attempt in 1997, the Canadian expedition made a conscious decision to climb via an alternative, easier route accessed via Nepal. Their thoughts, mindset, and experiences about the attempt are eloquently documented in a movie called *Above All Else*. The film is definitely worth seeing as it sheds light on parts of an expedition that are rarely seen but applicable to you right now as you build your practice—the tedious planning and logistics that take place before a climb and the countless run-throughs in the Canadian Rockies.

Interestingly, Hobson and Clarke both faced the exact same mental and physical challenges on that last trip but both describe it (and their internal approach) very differently. Both styles are poignant, powerful, and directly applicable to the challenges that you face right now in migrating all of your clients to a price based on the value you bring to the table.

Clarke, the consummate entertainer and passionate climber, doesn't take the climb too seriously and is often seen mugging for the camera.

He admits to feeling the fear and pressure but chooses not to focus on what could go wrong. Instead, he uses humor and his awe of the land-scape to preoccupy his mind so he can focus properly on the physical task at hand.

Hobson is much more reserved and measured. He wears the grav-ity of the situation and his trepidation on his sleeve. His face is serious and he pauses carefully to think about every question he is asked before responding. He is much more reflective and analyses each aspect of his thoughts, fears, beliefs, and perceived limitations in order to gain new, more empowering perspectives that will allow him to move forward with confidence. He is constantly breaking down his fears and looking at ways to reframe them in order to give himself the strength and resolve to keep going.

On the eve of the final push to the summit from Camp 4, we find both men literally exhausted and battling illness as the window of good weather begins to rapidly close. Their summit bid starts early the next day in complete darkness, with oxygen tanks. Early on, Hobson falls behind and contemplates giving up, only to be buoyed up and strengthened by the encouragement of his Sherpa.

Both successfully make it to the summit that day. However, their situation becomes grave on the descent when Hobson is on the verge of collapse because of problems with oxygen and the extreme cold. He openly recounts the concentration and resilience he had to muster in order to suspend fear while inching breathlessly across mile deep crevasses on rickety metal ladders, wearing awkward clamp-ons strapped to his boots and with 40 pounds of gear on his back.

He openly conveys the utter terror of hearing the mountain shift and thunder under his feet as they tread wearily beneath house-sized sheets of ice that he knew could fall down and crush them at any moment. Despite the odds against them, both Hobson and Clarke press on.

When confronted with the treacherous Khumbu Icefall, Clarke is asked, "Do you ever look down and think, my God, I cannot see the bottom?" And without hesitation he replied, "wherever you look or focus your attention on, that is exactly where you are going to end up. Looking down is incredibly dangerous. That is why I always focus my attention on where I need to get to and three steps ahead of where I am now."

And if you think about it, this advice alone is invaluable to you right now because if you are spending most of your time lamenting that you are too busy to learn HOW to Price Value or that you might lose clients, you aren't focusing on where you want or need to be. You are letting your fear and limiting beliefs cause you to look down to the bottom, which is exactly where you don't want to land.

Hobson and Clarke's personal account of their epic journey and the video footage of their chosen path hold deep insights and strategies that you can apply to your Pricing Value journey. But before we review the specific strategies that they used to control their fears, let's identify and examine what's holding you back right now and which insights from neuroscience can be brought to bear to give you leverage and inspiration to face your Everest—Pricing Value.

What Is Holding You Back?

Most of you have built your practice on hourly billing. That is because it has always been done that way and it is hard to break old habits, let alone wrap your head around the concept of "doing it another way."

So when you think about moving your clients to Pricing Value, what are some of the thoughts, ideas, beliefs, excuses, bad habits, and fears that come up for you?

What holds you back from converting 100 percent of them right now?

It's a confronting question, isn't it?

If you are still billing based on hourly or fixed pricing, there must be a reason for it. And that reason is most likely something within you—something causing you to delay or hesitate in making the shift.

Here is a list of the top worries, beliefs, reasons, and mindsets that accounting professionals most commonly give for not setting their price based on value:

- Fear of losing clients.
- Afraid of having to deal with price resistance and objections.
- Confusion around "how" to make the shift.
- Worry around not being good enough or "worth it."
- A belief that they are not good at sales.

- A belief that clients are primarily price conscious.
- Not having enough time to learn or implement a new way of pricing.

Now let's be honest, it's very common to have concerns, worry, or even fear around making the shift to Pricing Value. And to some extent, that fear is justified because it is not easy to implement it properly. If it were, everyone would have done it by now.

I'm sure you may even be willing to admit that from time to time you've experienced at least a handful of the common fears and excuses on this list. However, it's what you do next—after you have identified and acknowledged those concerns and fears—that will define your trajectory of success.

According to neuroscience, fear is simply the mind's way of letting you know that you MAY be in danger. Note the emphasis on the word "may" in that sentence. Remember, your brain is a survival mechanism whose sole purpose is to keep you safe and alive. Your brain uses fear to put things on your radar and give them heightened attention so you can take appropriate action to stay safe. Fear does not necessarily mean that you *are* in serious danger, it only means that you *may be*, and that you need to pay attention.

It's human nature to experience fear and equate that with a need to be cautious, to take one's time, and to make decisions that are likely to keep you safe/alive. It's quite another to let fear give rise to catastrophic thinking, shut down your senses and natural curiosity, annihilate your goals, and immobilize you so that you cannot move forward.

Fear is simply an emotion that the hardwired, automatic mechanism of your old brain uses to help keep you safe. But remember, it can only succeed in keeping you safe if you take action to move yourself out of harm's way. But if you choose to remain stuck and do nothing, you may actually put yourself in more serious danger unnecessarily.

Right now most of you are already under significant pressure with respect to your prices. Clients don't value what you do and often ask for a better price. Compound that pricing pressure with the reality that AI and machine learning are reducing the time it takes you to complete many of your compliance tasks. This means that there are fewer hours for you to bill each client. And if that weren't enough, you now know there is evidence to suggest your clients don't like hourly billing. Not only do they not like it, but also on a deeply subconscious level they actually equate it with pain. Truth is, your practice is in far greater danger right now if you do nothing than if you take action.

If fear is your primary motivator, most of you should have implemented Pricing Value yesterday. Thankfully, the second best time to do it is today.

So how are you going to take this information and apply it to tackle your fear as you move toward Pricing Value?

Your old brain is hardwired to make decisions automatically. As you discovered earlier, this part of your brain is very hasty and it relies primarily on visual cues for its information. Its sole function is to keep you alive—it's a survival-focused mechanism which means that if it perceives danger, it will act automatically to steer you away from that danger.

So here's the thing—no amount of thinking is going to override the survival mechanism of your old brain. Thinking kicks in after the survival mechanism has already decided or acted.

This makes the situation you are in right now very tricky as you cannot reason with or try to think your way out of fear. Unfortunately, you cannot rely solely on rational thought processes to deal with your fear around the move to Pricing Value.

This is going to sound counter-intuitive but the only proven way to overcome FEAR is exposure. Yes, you read that correctly—exposure.

Just like Hobson and Clarke, you must face what you fear and take action. Running from your fears never improves the way you think about them or the impact they have on your life. That is why most psychiatrists and psychologists recommend a version of this three step process to overcome fear:

1. Question your fears—many fears are based on false beliefs or catastrophic thinking.
2. Imagine the outcome that you want to have.
3. Face your fear(s).

Let's take this vital knowledge back now and examine how it played out for Hobson and Clarke and also draw some comparisons and conclusions on what you can do given the situation that you find yourself in right now.

Your Thoughts are More Powerful than Your Circumstances

Emotions, mindset, habits, self sabotage, worry, and fear have a tendency to creep in and permeate every aspect of your practice because your practice is simply just a natural extension of YOU. And if you have negative thoughts such as "I'm afraid I will lose clients" or "What if my clients object because they are primarily price conscious," then all of these thoughts, emotions, mindsets, and bad habits are already having a direct, and negative, impact on your results.

Your mindset is the unconscious driver that has put fear on the radar of your old brain. Therefore, if you can create some doubt in your negative beliefs, ideas, and so on, and arm yourself with some new, more resourceful perspectives about what your clients want and the upside potential, you will be well on your way to overcoming fear.

That is why the first and most important step in this process is to question you fears. Essentially you must ask, "What can I do to break down or disprove the assumptions/rules that prop up this fear?"

Hobson did this brilliantly. He took time to analyze each aspect of his thoughts, fears, beliefs, and perceived limitations in order to gain new, more empowering perspectives that allowed him to move forward confidently. He was also the one who got McIssac's two little girls on the satellite phone when he had lost his will to live. McIssac begged the team to leave him to die because he believed he could not make it back down the mountain. And yet when Hobson challenged this belief by introducing a new perspective (the promise he had made to his children), McIssac found the strength and was able to overcome both his fear and his dire medical condition.

Your thoughts are very powerful—more powerful than your circumstance, conditions, and concerns.

The second aspect of this process is imagining the outcome you want. Clarke said it best when he quipped, "Wherever you look or focus your attention on, that is exactly where you are going to end up. Looking down is incredibly dangerous." If you are being honest with yourself, isn't that exactly what you are doing right now—focusing on what you don't want? In order to engage the most powerful goal setting mechanism in the world, your brain needs to know exactly what you want.

Back in the 1960s, Dr. Maxwell Maltz discovered that the brain is a cybernetic system—a natural goal seeking mechanism—and operates just like the GPS on your car.[1] There is a part of your brain called the reticular activating system (RAS). It has several functions but the one that is most relevant to this discussion is its filtration system.

Every day you are bombarded with millions of bits of information per second. The RAS is the mechanism that deletes the vast majority of information from your conscious awareness so that you are not overwhelmed by all of this data. The RAS takes your beliefs, fears, and values, and so on, and uses that information to select what it filters out (discards) and what it presents to you.

Simply stated, your RAS is the radar or GPS that looks for and locates information, resources, and opportunities that will allow you to meet your goals. Like Clarke, if you want your mind to bring you solutions and to help you get to your end goals, you must invest time to put sufficient detail into your internal GPS. You need to take time to detail each particular element and wherever possible to use language or pictures to bring those specifics to life as your brain is a highly visual beast. Write down what it will look like when you achieve your goal and what you will be doing and saying when it comes to fruition.

And finally we come to the fun part…exposure.

You can learn a lot from Hobson and Clarke. They joined an expedition to climb one of the most difficult peaks in the world and they had almost no experience whatsoever. But they still did it and lived to tell the tale. However, if you go back and watch the documentary *Above All Else*, you will get an insight into all the hard work, training, and preparation that took place in the Canadian Rockies before they left. In Hobson's own words, "Success is 97 percent preparation and 3 percent execution." No truer words have ever been said.

---

[1] Dr. Maltz, M. 1960. *Psycho-Cybernetics*. California: Psycho-Cybernetics Foundation.

They didn't throw their hands up in the air and claim they were "too busy" to invest the time to learn and improve their skills. They made the decision they were going to summit Mt. Everest and they threw themselves in wholeheartedly. And now you must ask yourself, "What am I willing to give up in order to revolutionize my practice and bring more value to each client engagement?"

Take your time. Pricing and the semantics of pricing are the 3 percent—it's only the execution. To Price Value successfully, you must invest 97 percent of your time learning the skills you need to control your own fear, and master the value and leverage components.

Clarke and Hobson also learned the value of teamwork. They didn't try to do it all on their own (i.e., reinvent the wheel) or climb without oxygen. They found training and mentors (i.e., McIssac, the leader and one of the strongest climbers) within the expedition whom they could rely on for good advice and support. They took a different approach when their first two attempts up the North Face ended in disappointment. They didn't keep doing the same thing over and over and expect a different result.

And in the end, they found themselves in the position of being able to help their mentor (McIssac) to ignite his will to live, while they evacuated him off that mountain. You may want to ask yourself, "Am I trying to do this alone or am I open to learning a better way?"

Who is holding you accountable in your journey? Are you willing to let go of what didn't work in the past and be open to trying a different approach? Are you able to admit that you might need oxygen (i.e., practical strategies, skills, and a system)? Remember, controlling your own fear is just the first step to Pricing Value. It's what you do now—after you have identified and acknowledged those concerns and fears—that will define your trajectory of success.

Scaling Steep Slopes and Facing Fears

In many ways, we are all mountaineers. You do not need to travel to Nepal and climb Mt. Everest in order to prove your courage, as the mountain (disruption, technology, and unprecedented change) has already come to you. And you must climb in order to stay relevant and secure your livelihood.

No matter how steep the slope, how severe the terrain, or how punishing the elements and mental hurdles, the only thing left for you to do is to tie the knot in the rope (i.e., commit) and start climbing. We are all on this journey together. The future of our profession depends on your ability to redefine what it means to be an "accountant" by stepping up and delivering a whole lot more value to your clients.

CHAPTER 4

C#2 Comprehend Value

In 1949, 13 (out of a highly skilled team of 16 men) died battling a relatively small blaze that turned deadly in Mann Gulch, Montana. Upon investigating the circumstances of why 13 of the men died while only three lived, Norman Maclean wrote a book entitled *Young Men and Fire*, which is a true account of that fateful expedition of the "smoke jumpers"—firefighters who parachute into the back country to fight fires.

For those of you not familiar with the area, Mann Gulch is surrounded by steep canyon walls with the northern slope at a 75 percent incline. When the wind turned suddenly on the smoke jumpers that fateful day, they found themselves in a race for their lives up those steep walls in complete darkness and blazing heat.

One of the surprising and notable things that Maclean discovered was that the 13 who died had continued to carry their tools—poleaxes, saws, shovels, and backpacks weighing 44 lbs (20 kilograms)—while attempting to outrun the fire up those steep canyon walls. In other words, the 13 ran as far and as fast as they could with all their heavy equipment, even though that equipment was completely useless in a race against a raging fire up a steep slope.

Their inability to drop their heavy tools and backpacks ultimately prevented them from being able to outrun the fire. That single decision essentially cost them their lives.

Now you have to understand, to those seasoned firefighters, their tools were more than simple objects—they represented who they were, why they were there, and what they were trained to do. Dropping their tools would have meant abandoning all of their knowledge, beliefs, training, and experience.

While this might not seem like a hard choice to make to you right now, sitting in the comfort of your home or office, it represented an unfathomable predicament for those scared but brave young men. Unfortunately, these specialized firefighters hadn't been trained for such an unpredictable moment and they had no alternative models, strategies, or maps for behavior.

Interestingly, the three survivors of the blaze were forced to "think outside the box" and develop alternative methods to escape the fire. Once they figured out they were no longer "fighting the fire" but rather were "trying to escape from it," they realized they had to drop all of their useless equipment.

One survivor used an innovative technique called the "escape fire" where he took a match and lit a large ring of fire around himself and then crouched down on the ground under a blanket so that the fire would "jump" over him. When he tried to save the other men, they continued running right past him up the steep slope with all their gear on their backs because the "escape fire" technique was experimental and had not been part of their extensive training.

The inability of the 13 highly capable and experienced men to drop the equipment and tools that weren't working and seek new methods to escape is what ultimately led to them being engulfed by flames and smoke.

It begs the question: "What are the poleaxes, shovels, and backpacks you're currently trying to run with in order to implement Pricing Value?"

Are you willing to drop the tired, worn-out hourly and fixed price strategies, tools, and mindset which you are still lugging around?

What existing beliefs and models of behavior do you need to ditch in order for you to survive and prosper?

In the new world that you now find yourself in, the training, mindset, skills, approaches, and experience that got you to where you are now are not going to get you to where you need to be. That may sound harsh, but grasping this concept now is going to save you a whole lot of running around in the dark with stuff you don't need on your back dragging you down. In the realm of Pricing Value, your focus needs to be on the specific strategies and tools that will help you differentiate what you do, deliver real value, and render price a non-issue.

Putting Down the Beliefs, Tools, and Approaches that No Longer Serve You

The skills, mindset, and philosophy behind hourly rates and fixed packages are vastly different from those required to excel in Pricing Value.

The core distinction lies in whether you approach the client with the intent to first Comprehend Value or simply get clarity around the services that are requested.

One of the biggest mistakes accountants make when shifting from cost-based methods to Pricing Value is failing to do a proper 180 degree turn in both their approach and mindset. This failure to drop old tools and adopt the correct, new perspective is why most essentially end up with a fixed package (which is really just a derivative of hourly rates and cost-plus pricing).

Hourly Rates Approach

Figure 4.1 Your Approach When Charging by the Hour

When you approach your client with the intent to bill based on time, you lead with the services you can provide (see Figure 4.1). The very next thing that happens is the rate you quote is based on the amount per hour that you need to earn in order to cover all of your costs. As you can see, this approach is completely focused on you up until the time when you quote the rate. Your client can sense that they have not been taken into account and the most natural response from them is to balk at your price. Your client has no certainty around what this engagement will ultimately cost, and at a deeply unconscious level this feels unsafe.

To bring this back to our story about the smoke jumpers, this is exactly the point where the wind in your practice begins to pick up and you find yourself in a race against a raging fire of price objections up a steep slope with a pricing methodology that is about to kill your practice.

So what happens next? Some of you may get the bright spark that you need to make some changes so you drop a few heavy tools and make the decision that "you are going to put your client first" and adopt fixed packages as your methodology. But here's the thing…fixed packages are still backwards in terms of the approach and mindset. You may have less weight on your back but you are still trying to outrun the fire of constantly dealing with price objections.

Fixed Rate Approach

| Client | Service | Cost | Price | Value |

Figure 4.2 Your Approach When Charging a Fixed Price

While it may theoretically "put the client first" (because you have delivered certainty over what it will cost), your price is still essentially driven by your cost structures and the services that you want to offer. The price is still all about you and you haven't really involved the client in the process (see Figure 4.2). What you have done is first determined what it will cost you to deliver certain services and then marked them up to ensure that you make a profit. Yes, your client now has certainty over what this engagement will cost, but he or she still doesn't have value, which means you haven't outrun the fire of price objections. Your services are still not differentiated or valuable in your client's mind, which means they can easily look around, compare what you are offering to your competitors, and decide that you're just too expensive.

Yes, this approach is definitely superior to hourly billing but it still isn't Pricing Value, and that's a huge problem for you because it means you are still in a race against a raging fire of price objections up a steep slope.

The only way to survive is for you to create an "escape fire" by making the 180 degree shift to Pricing Value. When you make that decision, you must light a ring of fire around yourself, crouch down on the ground, and let the fire jump over you. What this means in practice is that you must put your client and what is of value to them first (that's the ring of fire). Next, you must crouch down and create enough value so that the fire of price objections essentially jumps over you and becomes a non-issue. You also need to stop running and put down the tools, mindset, and approaches that you have used in the past because they are completely useless to you now.

Pricing Value Approach

| Client | Value | Price | Solution | Cost |

Figure 4.3 Your Approach When Pricing Value

Pricing Value inverts the continuum completely—to prioritize the economic truth that your client is the ultimate judge of value (see Figure 4.3). What this means is that in the absence of understanding, quantifying, and acknowledging value up front, a value-based price cannot actually be set.

Unlike fixed or cost-plus pricing models, Pricing Value turns the order completely inside out. Your accounting services do not magically become more valuable because you have fixed the price or applied a markup to the costs involved so that you can make a profit. A firm committed to Pricing Value doesn't put themselves first, they put their clients first.

That's why it never makes sense to ask, "What price do we need to cover our costs and earn a profit?" However, if you are Pricing Value you might ask, "What costs can we afford to incur given the price we are able to secure from this particular client?"

Can you see the difference in those two perspectives?

And this is a really crucial distinction to make for another important reason. Most of you will already have a pretty good handle on your costs to complete certain tasks, hours spent by each team member, effort expended, efficiencies, risks, and other inputs. However, how much information do you measure and monitor around the value you actually create for your clients?

It's a confronting question, isn't it?

If you are now in the business of delivering value, when is now a good time to start tracking and keeping an eye on value?

Yes, the correct answer is now.

The truth is, clients are only willing to invest in solutions that solve pain points (the stuff that keeps them up at night or inspires them to achieve their desired transformations). That is why you must price the client and not the service. It all comes down to their pain points and their willingness to pay. In most cases, the value-based price will always be higher than hourly, fixed, or cost-based price because the value-based price is predicated on a custom, unique solution that cures key pain points and is higher in both actual and perceived value. It's the only solution where the fire of price objections jumps right over you and becomes a non-issue.

The client will always pay more money for value because the perceived impact to them and their business is much higher. In order to get to value, you need to stop putting your services and your costs first.

And if you think about it, most of what you do for your clients is focused on the numbers that describe the past and present of the business. Audits, financial statements, tax returns, and key performance indicators (KPIs) all help answer the basic question of what has transpired in the business to date. However, these compliance tasks are highly price sensitive, the scope of work is limited, and it is very difficult to get the client to see value in them.

In order to really create value for your clients, you must move away from a focus that is purely on your services and the costs required to deliver them. Instead you must shift toward curing the stuff that keeps your clients up each night worrying (or inspires them to achieve their dreams)—these hold the key to helping your clients move forward and they are the only thing that your client values.

But moving away from a focus on your services and the costs means that you need to deliberately put down the training, mindset, tools, and strategies that you have built your practice on and be open to learning new things. It means you need to stop telling your client how the engagement is going to proceed and start asking a lot more questions. Instead of controlling the relationship and the priorities, you are now entering the realm of collaboration.

Things are not as black and white in the realm of Pricing Value. In fact, you are about to discover there are a lot of shades of grey. Maybe not 50 shades of grey…but quite a few nonetheless.

Stop Guessing What Your Clients Want

Regardless of the specific service they approached you about today, every client is experiencing pain in some aspect of his or her business—these are the things that worry them and cause them to lose sleep at night or the contrast between where they are now and where they would like to be. Key pain points may include lack of cash flow, difficulty finding good staff, need for cost-effective ways to find more customers and boost sales, uncovering new ways to grow/innovate, lack of work-life balance, and productivity challenges. Curing these sources of pain is of enormous value to your clients and the key to Pricing Value is to weave in solutions to these pain points as part of the overall engagement that you propose.

Pricing Value is a holistic solution that uncovers and treats the root cause of pain (or desired transformation) in the business, not just the easy-to-spot symptoms the owner is aware of and came to you for help with.

But here's the thing...you cannot continue to guess or assume what your client needs and values. The tools that you've been using to onboard and price clients according to the services you provide and the price you need to get to make a decent profit, aren't going to back you into "what your client values." You need to find a system and tools that you can use to consistently and accurately uncover and quantify all of the pain points that your client values and is willing to pay you handsomely for the solution to.

How Do You Determine What Is of Value to Your Client?

To move into the domain of Pricing Value, you must master the skill of Comprehending Value—empowering your client to articulate, acknowledge, and quantify the extent to which these pain points are causing financial, strategic, or personal pain.

Financial pain is often about lack of results. Most clients will measure how they are doing by a KPI like cash flow, breakeven, cash gap, total sales, or return on equity (ROE). This will be the easiest stuff for you to work with as numbers are within your core competence and comfort zone. These are also the easiest to value since they are tangible, objective, and easy to measure.

Strategic pain is often more difficult to measure and quantify but is just as significant. It is usually tied to the way your client goes about producing, distributing, and selling products or services. To uncover strategic pain, you will want to explore business risk, quality issues, productivity, employee turnover, delivery challenges, supplier issues, market positioning, market share, branding, and so on.

Personal pain may reveal itself as work-life imbalance, difficulty sleeping, strained relationships, excessive stress, indecisiveness, bad habits, and fear of moving forward. Anything that relates to the feelings and emotions that your prospect has around their financial or strategic issues, and resolving them, will also fall under this heading. Pain in this realm can also present as a compelling goal or vision for the future that is so inspiring and all-consuming that it drives your client to snap out of complacency and take action to achieve it. This is the realm of transformation and it is much more difficult to quantify and may involve intangible or spiritual factors, which is why most in our profession ignore it completely. Getting to the bottom of this stuff can be messy—there are real emotions and leverage here, which is why it is so powerful in establishing trust between you and your client.

When your client opens up to you about all of their pain, you gain the most valuable power of all—leverage. Once you are armed with value and leverage, you have the two fundamental ingredients to master the art of Pricing Value.

So by now you must be wondering to yourself, "How (exactly) do I go about identifying and quantifying these pain points?"

To uncover and quantify pain (across all aspects—financial, strategic, and personal), you must ask open-ended questions such as:

- "What is the biggest challenge you are facing in your business?"
- "Why is that a problem for you?"
- "When your customer thinks of buying your product/service, what is the most difficult issue associated with acquiring it?"

It is crucial when asking these questions that you resist the urge to interrupt or prompt your client with suggestions. It is vital that you hear and understand what they are saying in their own words. Wherever possible, ask for permission to record the session with your client as it will free you up to be fully present. It is difficult to hear, understand, and actively listen when you are distracted by breaking eye contact to jot down what you are hearing. Simply let the client know that you want to capture their answers in their own words, that the recording will be treated as confidential and destroyed once you have had a chance to review it and extract what you need for your file notes.

And once you have identified the two to three most important pain points, you can then turn your mind to helping them quantify and acknowledge them. Regardless of whether the key pain points are financial, strategic, or personal in nature, it is crucial that you both understand what the value of the solution is and how motivated they are to cure each point (or achieve their desired transformation), before you move on further in the Pricing Value process. This step in the process should typically take 30 to 45 minutes, so slow down and take your time.

To put this in the language of our glass of water example from Chapter 1, you need to know whether your client is on a road trip with two screaming toddlers, in a Third World country, or dying of dehydration due to being stranded in the desert. You simply cannot afford to move on in the Pricing Value process until you fully comprehend the depth of your client's thirst.

*Please note—this is not the time for you to jump in and provide suggestions or solutions. Comprehending Value is about you taking the time up front to really understand what your client needs and values most. There will be plenty of time down the track to formulate and suggest solutions once the client has agreed to engage you. Right now, your sole focus is simply to Comprehend Value, not to cure it. You want to build up and understand the depth of your client's thirst, not let them off the hook with a tiny sip of water (or a whole glass) before they buy.

Why Is It So Important to Comprehend Value?

If you have done any reading or research on this topic, you will no doubt have come across the phrase "Price the client not the service." This catchphrase succinctly captures the essence of Pricing Value.

However, while concise and pithy, unfortunately it still leaves most a bit bewildered because it begs the question, "How does one go about pricing each client?"

In practical terms what this means is that you can no longer afford to guess what your client wants or needs, nor can you simply price a laundry list of all the services that your firm could provide. In order to price each client individually, you need to acquire new skills and change many aspects of your overall approach.

In particular, to Price Value you must get a whole lot better at the following:

- Asking questions that correctly identify and quantify the pain points of each client.

- Listening and responding with solutions to each pain point.
- Creating unique solutions that cure these specific pain points (including desired transformations).
- Realizing that pricing is an art form (it's subjective and there is no hard formula).
- Capturing and measuring the value you deliver.
- Communicating the value (verbal and non-verbal).
- Knowing your worth and also when you are prepared to walk away.
- Defining scope (and identifying scope creep).
- Understanding your firm's cost structure, efficiencies, effectiveness, risk, and so on.

Comprehending Value is the step that allows you to place the client (and what they need) first in your approach. It's the exact opposite of what you are doing right now. Executing this properly breaks the raging fire of price objections because you are involving your client in the process of determining how the engagement will cure the stuff that is keeping them awake at night. The price is driven by what is of value to them.

Failing to execute this properly means that what you are really doing is just trying to get the best price for your services and then trying to sell the value to your client at the end of the process. While it may work some of the time with some of your clients, you'll still be running from the fire of price objections on most days.

What Is Your "Escape Fire" Plan?

Unfortunately, the thinking and strategies that got you to here, won't get you to where you need to be. Never has the simplicity and wisdom of this statement been more poignant than it is today in our industry.

Those of you who adopt and learn the critical skills, tools, and mindset necessary to survive (and even thrive) will be the winners. This has always been true. Survivors and successful people triumph because they are agile, adaptable, and willing to do whatever it takes to get the results they desire and deserve.

Massive disruption and uncertainty necessitate a new perspective or innovative approach—the alternative, "doing the same thing over and over again," is the definition of insanity and can only lead to suffering, disappointment, and pain. If you do what you've always done to price your services, how can you reasonably expect a different result? If you are sick of price haggling and having your services treated as if they are indistinguishable from your competitors' services, then it is incumbent upon you to create an "escape fire" plan and execute it. Remember, any service can be differentiated and made special with a bit of work on your part.

In moments of uncertainty and imminent danger, clinging to the old "right" way might seem like a good idea. But more often than not, it may actually be deadly.

CHAPTER 5

C#3 Create Value

Creating Value is an elusive and often misunderstood concept because value is comprised of both tangible and intangible components. In order to maximize the value that you are able to create in the mind of your client, you must deliver the solution to their pain points AND manage their perception of value. Perception is a bit tricky because it may include a whole host of elements that are largely imperceptible and difficult to nail down. It's no easy task.

Thankfully, there are some proven, easy-to-implement strategies to help you navigate the subtle and not so subtle elements of Creating Value. We are going to start first with positioning—understanding why the physical price is often much less relevant than you think it is. Then we will move into how to deal with both tangible and intangible measurements and finish up with some little known techniques to help you influence your client's unconscious perception of value. These are invaluable because both science and psychology have actually proven that it is possible to significantly influence a client's perception of your price without changing the actual dollar amount.

In many ways, the perception of value in your client's eyes is equally as (if not more) important than tangible value. Unfortunately, perception of value is the single most overlooked factor in our industry. Nailing both tangible value and perception of value has the potential to differentiate you from 99 percent of your peers. And differentiation is lucrative both in terms of the prices you can command, and also your ability to attract and retain a much higher calibre of client.

Positioning—How to Make Price a Non-Issue

It has often been said that "when the true cost of a problem is fully uncovered, the price of the solution frequently becomes irrelevant."

In order to Price Value, you must help your client identify, quantify, and acknowledge the true cost of their pain points. Without this integral component, you will fall prey to arguments based on price. If you are currently struggling with clients who don't value your work or expect a discount, it all comes down to this one simple point—you haven't taken enough time up front to uncover the true cost of continuing to do nothing. You are still pricing the work based on outputs/services you offer, and the client doesn't value them highly. (Please also refer back to Chapter 4 for a discussion of how to uncover the true cost of their pain points.)

In a nutshell, you are your own worst enemy and have created the situation where your clients have become price conscious. The good news is that with one powerful shift in the way that you approach Creating Value, you can turn this around and start attracting and experiencing clients who are predominately value conscious.

Here's an example that you should be able to relate to…

Twelve months ago, Alan would have fought vehemently to defend his belief that ALL of his clients were price conscious. And to be fair, most of them probably were, but only because he taught them to be.

Alan has practiced as a tax accountant for nearly 15 years and he has built a very busy practice with eight other accountants and four book-keepers working under him. Because his practice is software agnostic, they have a diverse mix of clients from various industries. Alan is known for being a no-nonsense kind of guy and he gets most of his new clients by referral.

There was only one problem. Alan had always invoiced the work based on hourly rates, billed each client quarterly, and given most of them 30 or more days to pay. He had a deeply ingrained belief that his clients would walk if he tried to implement value-based billing or fixed packages. This belief was solidified by his anecdotal evidence that his clients often took too long to pay and quibbled about the price.

Unfortunately, all of this was compounded by the fact that he tried to institute fixed packages with a handful of his clients, and it was a disaster. It took him ages to get the new plans in place and in some cases he found that he was actually already nine months into the new taxation year before he got the agreements in place and commenced monthly billing.

As you can imagine, this had a horrific impact on his cash flow, and he got a bit disillusioned by the whole thing.

His clients couldn't see any difference between what they got under the fixed packages vs. the previous year, and as you can well imagine, they didn't hold back in telling him they weren't too happy. The cash flow crunch and the knock-backs from clients really hurt Alan's confidence and further entrenched the belief that value-based pricing could not possibly work for his practice because his clients were "far too price conscious."

Does any of this sound familiar?

It should, because "it won't work for me...my clients are too price conscious" is one of the top three reasons why accountants procrastinate and delay moving away from hourly rates. The fear of losing clients or having to deal with price objections are formidable mental obstacles for most of you.

But the truth is, no two products or services are identical. Even small differences between similar products or services can make price a non-issue. This is especially true if those differences tie directly to multiple elements of the client's problem in a way that makes the solution that you offer seem like the ONLY sane one.

In order to help you understand this concept at a deeper level, let's look at an example which is not too dissimilar from the position that you find yourself in right now...

On the surface, it may often appear that two B2B solutions perform an identical function—that is, have the same features and benefits and are therefore interchangeable in the mind of the client. This interchangeability is exactly what drives the need to compete on price because the client has no other way to distinguish the difference. Commoditization creates the need to discount.

However, in reality, no two competitive B2B solutions are ever exactly alike, and it is those differences that hold the potential to create wildly different perceptions and value. As the provider of a service to business owners, it's your job to uncover the pain points and perceptions that will cause price to become insignificant and leave your solution as the only logical choice.

Imagine for a moment that there are two order processing systems that have the same features and benefits, but one has a price that's half as much as the other. In the absence of any other factors, the price-focused customer is probably going to choose the lower priced system, right?

However, what if the lower priced system goes offline or has bugs three times more often than the higher priced system? And what if the employees of the price-focused purchaser find themselves in an unenviable position where they can't do their jobs properly (i.e., place orders for clients) because the lower price system goes down a lot during the workday? If the outages result (or have the potential to result) in a loss of sales in the thousands or even millions, this factor alone could immediately disqualify the lower priced system as a contender with potential purchasers.

Think about the cloud accounting software and other apps you use right now. Some of them are more reliable than others, aren't they? What happens when you cannot access the government portal to file a tax return or when the bank feeds are not correct in your client's accounting software package? Some vendors have fewer bugs and downtime. Some have great support (online and via telephone), while others can take days to get back to you.

In B2B sales, almost every unique solution has some Economic Value above and beyond the value of the time and materials that went into delivering it. If you want to Price Value masterfully, your job is to uncover the Economic Value in your proposed solution and present it in such a way that your client can easily understand why your price is justified and your solution is the only sane option.

But what (exactly) is Economic Value? That is a great question.

Economic Value is the total monetary worth of your offer, from the customer's perspective. It stems from your core service plus the insights, impact, ease of access, functionality, response time, quality, and support, and so on, that are provided before, during, and after the sale.

However, because your client is not the expert, it is your job to help them SEE how your offering creates this Economic Value by improving their results/performance, reducing their overall costs, and/or reducing their exposure to risk and liability.

As you have already discovered, the majority of business purchases are made to solve some sort of pain point, for example, productivity problems, delivery problems, quality problems, cash flow, employee retention, work-life balance, loss of market share, gap between where they are vs. where they would like to be and so on. These pain points consume significant time and resources for your clients which creates unnecessary costs within their organization.

Depending on the size and sophistication level of your client, they may—or may not—be aware of the true economic impact of these problems. Therefore, as you discovered in the last chapter, the first step in this process is to identify and quantify the problem your client is working to resolve. The second step is to determine how much this problem is actually costing them. In most cases, you are looking for accurate dollars-and-cents figures where the pain is financial. Where the pain is personal or strategic in nature, you will need to work harder as the costs may be intangible or more difficult to quantify (but significant nonetheless).

Next, you must uncover the root cause(s) of the client's problem. Having this knowledge will enable you to provide a long-term solution that will create more Economic Value for them. The client will always pay more for the solution, as opposed to a mere band-aid for the symptoms. Having all of this information will allow you to Create Value by helping your client address these root cause(s), either with your services alone or with a combination of your services and additional information, technology, or third party services and support.

The best way to create Economic Value is by asking questions that gradually reveal the true cost of your client's problems. In this context, questions are in fact the answers.

Note, this approach is fundamentally different from the traditional sales process many of you are familiar with and inherently dislike—where you are encouraged to do most of the talking to present features and benefits, overcome objections, and then "close the deal." There is a reason that the traditional approach feels "icky" and incongruent—you are an accountant not a used car salesman. Your job is not to "sell your clients" on anything. Your role is to help them fully understand what the problems actually cost them, and reveal enough Economic Value in your proposed solution so that price becomes a non-issue and it's easier for them to say "yes."

With Pricing Value, you focus primarily on crafting questions that will uncover areas where he or she does not yet understand the cost of a problem. As you do so, you'll uncover areas of great Economic Value that the customer may not even realize…and which ideally will tie to something unique about your solution. What you are looking for are opportunities to Create Value in what you offer—aspects of your solution that make it far more valuable than merely the time or materials that went into creating it.

To do this, your conversation with your client should cover:

- Revenue, bottom line or cash flow.
- Reducing costs.
- Quality improvement.
- Delivery performance or customer service.
- Reduced exposure to risk and liability.
- Personal pain points and/or their vision (or desired transformation).

And remember our accountant Alan from earlier in this chapter? This is exactly where his pricing journey went off the rails.

When discussing the engagement with a new or existing client, he focused almost exclusively on the tasks at hand—in most cases the reason they came to him for help was their tax return. And if you think about it, the tax return is not a differentiated product. The client doesn't see or perceive great Economic Value in the preparation of that return because it is simply something that they need to do in order to comply with the tax regime. It doesn't put more money in their bank account, improve the efficiencies of their business, or help them to grow in any way.

No matter what Alan did, as long as he continued to focus on the tax return itself, he always got the same result. Even if Alan was brilliant at his job and successful at minimizing their tax, the client still saw the task as undifferentiated and was understandably price conscious. They had a hard time distinguishing between the work that Alan did and what any other competent accountant down the road could offer.

To succeed at Pricing Value, Alan had to change his approach completely and spend a lot more time comprehending their pain points and establishing more Economic Value in his offer—the specific and perceived value that he could offer, which went above and beyond the time and materials required to produce the tax return. By asking better questions, he was able to uncover a number of pain points and deal breakers that greatly enhanced the scope of value he could propose.

He discovered that many clients wasted a lot of time gathering and organizing paper receipts. Many had at least one aspect of their return (i.e., claiming home office expenses or vehicle allowances) that put them in a high risk bracket for audit. Understandably, the risk, cost, and stress associated with being singled out for an audit was a major pain point. In addition, quite of few of them were in the technology space and were keen to get their returns completed quickly at the end of year in order to apply for and get their R&D tax credit back as soon as possible.

Knowing these insights was a huge advantage for Alan because it meant he could now present a solution that had a lot more Economic Value for each client. Instead of just pricing the tax return at a fixed amount, he could easily present a small selection of packages that incorporated the Economic Value of turning the return around in less than two weeks, providing a receipt scanning app that saved on average eight hours a month of the owner's time, and audit insurance which mitigated a huge risk and gave the owner much more peace of mind.

That is why this step is so powerful—it allows you to clearly define the Economic Value of your solution to your client in a way that makes it difficult or impossible for a competitive offering (or doing nothing) to seem like a sane option. Through this process, you must uncover the deal-breakers (like the costly downtime in the software solution example or the risk of audit that Alan's clients feared) that create real Economic Value in the eyes of your client. Economic Value is old-brain friendly—it makes it a no-brainer for your client to say "yes" and step into the solution today. They don't have to do a whole lot of thinking to process your message and waste both energy and time in the process.

It's the Economic Value—which proceeds directly out of this differentiation process—that renders price a non-issue in the eyes of your client. If your client objects to the price, there is a strong likelihood that you have not yet created enough Economic Value in your proposal. You then know it's time to go back to the drawing board and devise more questions to draw out the major impediments and deal-breakers.

Creating Tangible versus Perceived Value

To Create Value, you must manage both tangible and intangible (perceived) factors. Tangible factors include the measurable costs that you have quantified with your client by going through the process of Comprehending Value that we discussed in the previous chapter. Intangible or perceived factors may also be uncovered in this questioning process and include (but may not be limited to):

- Personal pain.
- Strategic pain and spiritual factors.
- Client's overall perception of your service.
- Subtle but powerful pricing cues that are often undetected by the conscious mind.

The tangible stuff is somewhat easier as it can often be pointed to, measured, and monitored. It's also within your comfort zone to deal with numbers. The intangible stuff is much trickier because you are dealing with someone else's perception AND the goalposts can shift from time to time. Let's take a quick look at a few of the intangible factors that increase the perception of value. When you embark on Pricing Value, you must manage both, but often it's the intangible factors that 99 percent of accountants and bookkeepers will misinterpret, misjudge, or miss completely.

Boosting Value and Price Simultaneously

In the accounting industry, the way you introduce new prices can make a huge difference to both how they are accepted by your clients and how they impact the bottom line of your practice. The key to success in Pricing Value is to show greater value along with your new price based on that value. In fact, many reputable studies have proven that if the change in price (whether a change in hourly rates or a move from hourly to a value-based price) is not supported by an increase in both value and perceived value in the eyes of the client, it will be rejected.[1]

While a small percentage do focus on price alone, research supports the view that most clients consider the balance of both value and price.[2] If you can clearly demonstrate you're offering more in terms of Economic Value and perceived value, a price increase may virtually go unnoticed. This is a very important distinction and it goes to the heart of what Pricing Value is truly about. It's easy to get caught up in the fact that you will now be charging a higher amount but it is crucial to remember that this comes with a responsibility to create and deliver more value to your client.

With great reward also comes great responsibility.

Influencing the Perception of Value

The price you charge must be supported by the value and perceived value in your service. It is not as simple as "just switching from hourly to value pricing." All too often we see vendors and accountants telling us that they start with the client and what is of value to them but what becomes apparent when you dig deeper is really a focus on services (and the costs to deliver them) being used as the primary proxy to determine price. It's not enough to say you "start with the client and value in mind"—you must execute it seamlessly in practice.

Clients base perceived value on reference points. If you're selling a service, most will look around and find another service to compare yours to. If that search uncovers that your competitor sells it for $200, then this will impact their overall perception of the "right price" for the service.

---

[1] "Reflection on a Price Increase." 2017. *Pippin's Plugins*, March 21, 2017, https://pippinsplugins.com/reflection-on-a-price-increase/ Also, Dr. Lee, N. 2017. "'Why Pay?': Cracking the Code for Communicating Price Increases." *State of The Conversation Report*. Warwick Business School.

[2] Leszinski, R., and M.V. Marn. 1997. "Setting Value, Not Price." *The McKinsey Quarterly*, February 1997, www.mckinsey.com/business-functions/marketing-and-sales/our-insights/setting-value-not-price

If your generic service is more expensive than the common reference points in your industry, you will need to take demonstrable action to change the perception of the category or the uniqueness and value that your solution provides.

If your solution is at the leading edge, highly specialized/relevant, or disruptive, there may be no clear price reference. That is why having strong Economic Value is crucial to your success in Pricing Value. If you can achieve it, prospective clients are much more likely to accept the price that you determine.

Therefore, if you want to Price Value in your accounting practice, you must either create a new category or deliver a solution that is so unique (highly specialized and relevant) that it cannot easily be duplicated by your competition. This is another reason why it is imperative to niche down. The more expertise you have in a particular niche, the greater the likelihood you can create solutions that immediately disqualify your competition.

To execute this masterfully, you should be asking yourself, "What can I become the BEST in the world at?"

Context Sets Perception

Imagine that your friend is helping you move house on a sweltering day. Your friend offers to go out and grab a six-pack of beer at the shops nearby, but before doing so casually asks, "What's the most you're willing to pay for the beer?"

Seems like a fair question, doesn't it?

Of course the context of time, location, and how thirsty you are impacts your price sensitivity. In fact, a situation very similar to this was explored in depth by Richard Thaler.[3]

His team tested two scenarios. In the first, the friend went to get beer from a local run-down grocery store. In the second version, he frequented a 5-star hotel down the street and ordered it from the bar. However, the ambiance of the hotel was irrelevant in this test, as the beer was purchased and taken offsite to be consumed.

---

[3] Thaler, R. 1983. "Transaction Utility Theory." *Advances in Consumer Research 10*, pp. 229–32.

Thaler discovered that subjects agreed to pay more if they were told that the beer was being purchased from an exclusive hotel. On the face of it, this seems to violate the basic principle that a six-pack of Coronas is worth a certain amount and no more.

What it does suggest, however, is that customers do in fact take cues from their surroundings when making price-related decisions. Humans expect to pay more for a cold beverage when it is dispensed by a waiter behind an ornate, hand-carved, solid wood bar. Similarly, consumers will happily pay more for produce in an upscale, whole foods environment, but they might balk at the same price per pound if they saw it in their local grocery store.

When introducing Pricing Value, this research advocates that it's important to pay attention to the environment where you make your offer to your prospect or client. Whether it be on your website, a sales presentation in your boardroom, a casual lunch or via an online platform (Skype, Zoom), your client's perception of value is likely to be highly influenced by their surroundings. If you want to command a premium price, the context in which your offer is presented must be congruent with luxury and significance.

Bundling

Every single time your client sees another individual charge (or hours) racking up, their old brain (i.e., the survival mechanism) equates these increments with pain. Reducing everything to one single charge each month means less pain to the part of the brain that decides, which is a good thing. It also makes mental price comparisons much more difficult, as individual prices are concealed.

Take this common scenario for example... $500 might seem like a lot of money for search engine optimization, but when it's part of a $5,000 website overhaul that includes a new WordPress theme, copyediting, custom photos, blog posts, social media training, search engine optimization, and several other items, it becomes much more difficult to judge the price or value of any single component.

This technique is often expertly employed by restaurants selling à la carte items (i.e., sushi). To combat the perceived pain of piece-by-piece pricing, many have adopted innovative strategies under the theme of bundling. For example, it is very common to see rows and rows of combination platters and pre-packed assortments. These contain a variety of sushi items for one simple price.

Two innovative sushi restaurants, Yo! Sushi and Roll On, even went so far as to eliminate prices (almost) completely. Instead of prices, each item is associated with a colored dot that corresponds to a price on a legend at the bottom of the menu. So, as you select each item from their menu, you aren't confronted with the cost of each piece.

Even though much of the research around this concept has been done outside our industry, you can still use it to your advantage. For instance, you may consider removing individual pricing and avoid itemizing the prices for every service that you offer on your website and in your marketing materials. Rather than sell individual services at an hourly or fixed rate, it makes good sense for you to offer a packaged bundle at a price that includes a combination of things that must be done plus the solutions to the client's key pain points. The client can then choose, from a few options, which specific bundle best suits his or her needs and priorities. This approach squarely focuses the client on priorities and deflects attention away from price.

Establish New Service Options

And finally, you may want to consider expanding your service options to include items that are of specific Economic Value to your ideal clients. For instance, if you are like Alan and some of your clients could benefit from a quicker turnaround, you may want to introduce premium pricing for instant, same day, or overnight service. The same principle applies to catch up or rescue jobs. Unfortunately, many of you undervalue yourself when pricing these sorts of engagements because you assume that the client will not be willing to pay for the amount of time it really takes to get the work done properly. That sort of thinking has no place in a firm that Prices Value. The Economic Value is not in completing the task itself but in the relief your client will get from knowing where they stand, complying with federal or state tax requirements, and avoiding fines, audits, or jail terms.

CHAPTER 6

C#4 Capture Value

Have you ever noticed that there are a lot of people in the accounting industry telling you that all you need to do is put up your hourly rates or move to fixed pricing, and all your problems will be solved?

Well, Dan did exactly that and the end result almost cost him his practice.

When it was just Dan and his overheads were low, everything was fine. He made a decent income. He was like so many sole practitioners, based out of a home office with a reasonable portfolio of clients.

But as his practice began to grow, his hours just got longer and longer until he was working seven days a week and was exhausted. So he decided the easiest way to cope with all the extra work was to hire staff and increase his hourly rate by 15 percent. And with the extra staff came the need to train and track what they were doing, and move to an office that could accommodate the entire team. Before he knew it, Dan's revenue was falling far short of what was required to cover the rent and all the salaries.

So, Dan took the advice of an "expert" and devised a plan to hike up his prices by 45–50 percent for every client. However, this time he accomplished the increase by moving his clients from hourly rates to fixed packages using a proposal app from the ecosystem. Initially, he was amazed how many clients stayed with him, and how easy it had been to "just put up his prices." He thought to himself, "Why didn't I do this sooner?"

But the honeymoon period didn't last very long. It started with just one or two clients leaving at first. Over a six-month period, almost 47 percent of his client base was eroded yet he was still left with an office and team members that he couldn't support with his reduced billings. Dan was perplexed because he thought he had done everything right. He followed the advice he was given "to a T" and the proposal software had made it very easy for him to increase the amount he was charging for his services.

All of his old and new clients seemed happy to pay the new rates and Dan continued to give the same thorough and conscientious service that he had always given. He could not understand where he went wrong.

And therein lies the problem, not just for Dan, but also for you as you embark on this journey. If you attempt to Capture more Value from your clients, without simultaneously putting a plan in place to create and deliver more value, you will fail. Even if you enjoy short-term gains in the beginning, over time, you will often find that they are short-lived.

Creating Value for your clients is just the beginning of the Pricing Value journey. If you want to remain in business and build a successful practice that endures, you must also learn how to Capture Value correctly for your firm. Just as Dan discovered the hard way, there is a lot more to growing a successful practice than you focusing solely on what you need to get. You may recall from Chapter 4, it's not as simple as putting your prices up or using an app to re-price all of the services that you want to provide. You must shift your mindset 180 degrees—move away from a focus that is purely on your services and the costs required to deliver them, and toward curing the stuff that keeps your clients up at night.

In a nutshell, Capturing Value is the process by which you retain a percentage of the value you create and deliver to your clients. For example, if the work you do with your client leads to incremental revenue (or savings) of $1 million, and you charge $100,000, you've captured 10 percent of the Value Created. To successfully Price Value in your practice, you need to:

• Understand, create, measure, and deliver value.
• Communicate it in a way that is easy for your client to say "yes" to.
• Capture a fair share of that value for your firm.

Like Dan, for those of you who bill based on hourly or fixed rates, you are shooting yourself in the foot because you are not Capturing Value. Even if you think your "fixed price" compliance services are close enough (or very similar) to "value-priced," you are deluding yourself.

Now some of you may be sitting there thinking to yourself, "Why does it even matter? As long as I make a good profit, isn't that enough?"

and "If I am making more profit than before and creating more value for my clients, haven't I accomplished the most important goal behind Pricing Value in the first place?"

And those are really great questions to have, because this very point has been debated by some of the most prominent business minds in the world, and they have ALL come to the exact same conclusion.

Successful businesses are valuable only because they have mastered the art of Capturing Value. Creating massive value alone, is not enough—in fact, several businesses that have created billions of dollars of value for their customers still went under because they failed to Capture Value for themselves.

The Relationship Between Creating and Capturing Value

According to Peter Thiel, co-founder of PayPal and author of *Zero to One*, "All happy companies are different: each one earns a monopoly by solving a unique problem. On the other hand, all failed companies are the same: they failed to escape their competition."[1]

One of Peter's favorite (contrarian) questions is: "What valuable company is nobody building?"

So you may be asking yourself, "What relevance does this question have to the topic of Pricing Value in my accounting practice?"

And the answer to your question is: "Nothing…and yet everything."

You see Thiel defines a valuable company as one that both Creates Value and Captures Value.

Now to be fair, Peter's question is a lot more complicated than it looks because right now your practice could theoretically create a lot of value without actually becoming valuable itself. Unfortunately, Creating Value is never going to be enough—success and longevity are reserved for those of you who simultaneously capture some of the value that you create for your clients.

---

[1] Thiel, P.A., and B. Masters. 2014. *Zero to One: Notes on Startups, or How to Build the Future.* New York, NY: Crown Business.

The relationship between Creating Value and Capturing Value is incredibly complex because:

- You can Create Value without capturing any of it.
- You cannot Capture Value without first creating it.
- It is possible to Capture more Value while simultaneously creating less.

Clear as mud, right?

Sorry, perhaps fair warning should have been given that we are about to dive down the rabbit hole together, in true Alice in Wonderland style. Oh well, now that we are here, we might as well proceed.

At the moment, you find yourself in the middle of a perfect storm. Competition, access to information, and the fast pace of technological advancement are putting pressure on you to close the link between Creating Value and Capturing Value. Less than 2 percent of firms understand and have correctly responded to these perilous market forces.

When competition is high, you inevitably get put under pressure to discount your charge-out rates. The direct impact of this is less value created for clients and less cash flow secured by you. And for those of you who are charging via fixed or hourly rates, no value is captured whatsoever. Both sides lose.

The correct response to these pressures is the exact opposite of what you are currently doing. In a highly competitive market, your job is to increase profit, cash flow, and market share through Creating Value. And once you have created that value, your survival is based on your ability to capture a large percentage of it. This requires a delicate balancing act.

If you try to Capture more Value, like Dan with his price increase (whether via fixed or hourly rates), without Creating more Value for your clients, you will lose clients to your competitors. And if you fail to capture a decent chunk of the value you create for your clients, your practice is virtually worthless—that is because your firm is only as valuable as the amount you are actually able to capture.

Value Capture Has Many Enemies

Unfortunately, the process of Capturing Value has many enemies: competition and commoditization, reinvestment and technological obsolescence, fluctuating revenue and churn, and piss poor execution. And as has often been said, "There are no real winners in business, only survivors." You can't always outrun all of the impediments to Capturing Value but you do a lot to pull out and stay ahead of the pack, and in the process differentiate yourself from 98 percent of your competitors who are still making no attempt to Capture Value.

Competition and Commoditization

Right now, your practice creates $X value for your clients and captures Y percent of that value. However, what is important to note is that X and Y are independent variables. In fact, they are completely autonomous. Just because you create significant value for one or more of your clients doesn't mean that you are capturing a large percentage of it for your firm or yourself. Contrary to popular belief amongst accountants, profitability is not the primary determinant of value for your firm.

Just as Dan found out when fixed costs escalated when he hired staff, profitability reflects your ability to earn revenue relative to your internal cost structure and efficiencies. The margin that you earn is merely a percentage that you retain from the revenue you charge your clients. If you charge based on hourly or fixed rates, your revenue is in no way tied to the value that you have created for your clients. In fact, it is solely a function of your own costs and competence in getting the job done. Any attempts by you to improve your firm's profitability will not result in the increased value of your firm. You cannot increase the value of your firm unless you Capture Value based on what you have created and delivered for your clients.

This is precisely why even very large and long-standing businesses can still be "bad" businesses by Thiel's definition. Take any one of the US airline carriers, for example. Each year they service millions of passengers, create hundreds of billions of dollars in revenue, but only generate 0.2

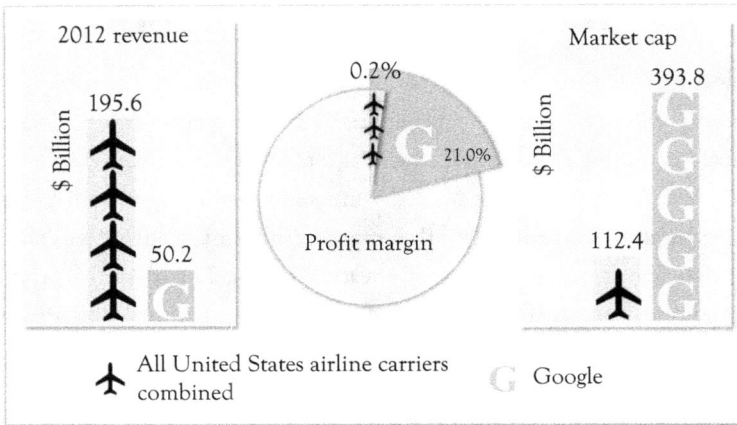

Figure 6.1 Value Capture Comparison

percent net profit (see Figure 6.1). With revenue in total of $195.6b, the collective market capitalization of all carriers only amounted to $112.4b.[2]

On the flip side, there are a number of notable high quality companies that capture a huge percentage of the value that they create for their clients/customers. Take Google for example. Google grossed only $50b during that same time period but managed to retain 21 percent of that as profit and was valued at $393.8b (roughly 3.5 times the value of all US airlines combined).

Google is much more effective at Capturing Value than all of the well-established businesses in the airline industry. But why is Google so much better at Capturing Value?

The answer is: because it has effectively created a monopoly for itself on search. In fact, they are so good at what they do, they have all but eliminated the other competitors from contention. A firm subject to strong competitive forces for their undifferentiated product/service must sell at a market price—that is unavoidable. Since Google owns the market, it has earned the right to set its own prices.

---

[2] Jorgenson, E. 2015. "Why Value Capture Is the Most Important Business Idea You Haven't Read Enough About." *Evergreen*, https://medium.com/evergreen-business-weekly/why-value-capture-is-the-most-important-business-idea-you-haven-t-read-enough-about-c035c657d091

The lesson for you as you look to future-proof your practice is this—it is impossible to Create and Capture lasting Value if you continue to insist on building an undifferentiated service-based practice and billing based on your costs. In order to master the step of Capturing Value, you must first take a step back and examine what business you are in. And once you have done that you can come back to the drawing board and start to put the building blocks in place to differentiate your practice and stand out in the marketplace, in order to earn the right to set your prices accordingly. When you can set your own price based on the value that you bring to the table, you will start to Capture Value and begin to future-proof your practice.

Reinvestment and Technological Obsolescence

This is such an important lesson for you on the topic of Capturing Value that it makes sense to bring in the big guns.

Warren Buffett learned the hard way how reinvestment and technological obsolescence can be the enemy of Capturing Value. Since Buffett is arguably the leading business and investment advisor in the world, what he learned after acquiring a textile manufacturing business in decline is well worth paying attention to. Several decades ago, a loom manufacturer approached him with an revolutionary invention that promised to do twice as much work as the old loom his plant was using. Buffet famously retorted "Gee, I hope this doesn't work because if it does, I'm going to close the mill."

Now many of you may be confused with that statement but Buffet understood that the textile business was in fact a lousy business. They were earning poor returns and it simply did not make sense to invest enormous amounts of capital into a terrible business. Buffet grasped better than most, that the huge productivity increases that they might reap from the new loom to produce a commoditized product, would only flow on to the buyers of the textiles. Both the buyers of the product and the sellers of the equipment stood to gain vast amounts of value, but he knew that he would not reap any of the benefit as the owner of the manufacturing plant. In Buffet's own words "nothing was going to stick to our ribs as owners."

Here's the problem…

When companies want to sell you new equipment or technology, they always show you projections of the savings that you will reap based on current prices. Unfortunately, this is only half the story. What they often fail to disclose, or choose to sweep under the carpet, is the amount of the benefit that will stick to your ribs vs. how much will instead flow on to your customer or client. What happens is that you can easily get talked into buying equipment or technology that supposedly will pay for itself in 2–3 years, but what you will find, is that your margins continue to be lousy.

Charlie Munger recounted some of Buffett's key insights at the USC Business School back in 1994. And since his message on how tough it is to Capture Value is so powerful and poignant, it's best to hear that message exactly as it was delivered by him.[3]

> *And it isn't that the machines weren't better. It's just that the savings didn't go to you. The cost reductions came through all right. But the benefit of the cost reductions didn't go to the guy who bought the equipment.*

Not all reinvestment is bad investment. However, it pays to be able to discern which scenario you currently find yourself in.

Right now you are in a market where most of what you do is viewed by your clients as indistinguishable from your competitors and you are primarily being paid by the hour. As AI and machine learning automate more and more of these tasks, the benefit will be captured by the technology vendors and your clients. In Buffett's vernacular, none of it is going to "stick to your ribs" as the accountant.

This is a huge risk because as we discussed earlier, the amount you can charge for pure compliance work is decreasing. Surviving on less cash flow each year makes you vulnerable to price-based competition and changes

---

[3] Munger, C.G. 1994. "A Lesson on Elementary, Worldly Wisdom as It Relates to Investment Management & Business," *Y Combinator*, https://old.ycombinator.com/munger.html

in market conditions, and it robs you of your ability to reinvest in yourself and your team to gain competitive advantage.

Capturing Value is actually vital to your survival because it allows you to reinvest in training, R&D, and other initiatives to create a stronger competitive advantage. However, to achieve this you must clearly deliver something so differentiated and desirable to your ideal client that it disqualifies every other accountant. Else, you risk ending up in the exact same predicament that Buffett found himself in—pouring blood, sweat, and tears into a practice that will never be saleable (i.e., of significant value), because you haven't found a way to Capture Value for yourself.

Fluctuating Revenue and Churn

Long gone are the days when the number of clients in your stable and goodwill were taken into account in determining practice value. In the modern world of accounting, your ability to Capture Value is the primary contributor to the value of your practice. Value is often measured as a function of your pricing power, reliable revenue, cash flow, and churn.

Unfortunately, not all revenue is created equal. In addition to being able to capture a large percentage of the value you create for your clients, revenue quality and predictability are now also very important. Remember how Google's valuation was significantly better than that of the US airlines, even though revenue was much lower?

Monthly recurring revenue (MRR) is now one of the primary drivers of value in your practice. MRR is the total amount that your clients pay up front each month as an agreed amount. MRR is really valuable for five reasons:

- It's predictable, which makes it far easier to use for forecasting and growth purposes. Hourly billings can change widely each month but MRR usually doesn't.
- It's much more scalable—your administration costs are lower, no time wasted on timesheets and debt chasing.
- It forces accountability and interaction with your clients as you are on the hook to deliver value every single month.
- Your client has control, choice, and certainty over what it will cost, which is old-brain friendly.

- Because it's a monthly amount, it can be reviewed easily
  and often by both you and the client to ensure that they are
  getting everything they need and value. It can also be updated
  quickly, which is not the case for annual rates.

Another crucial factor is of course switching costs (churn). This too has changed significantly in our industry in the past five years.

Long gone are the days when clients stayed with one accountant forever. Technology has actually made it easier for your clients to switch accountants and in some cases clients are even choosing accountants now based on the technology the new accountant uses. As it becomes easier and easier for your clients to leave you, it weakens your ability to Capture Value. Your ability to differentiate what you do and create stickiness is the only antidote to churn. And statistically speaking, companies (across all industries) with churn rates of less than 5 percent annually are more likely to have price to revenue multiples on valuation in the top 10 percent of their industry.

This has further implications for you as you move to implement Pricing Value. In most cases, your clients will be paying monthly. Because clients are often not locked into long-term service agreements, you must work even harder to manage how you create and deliver value to them. The longer the client stays with you, the more pricing power you have, which enhances your ability to Capture Value.

It's a delicate balancing act—improving the quality of your revenue by implementing MRR and simultaneously managing churn (due to lower switching costs).

Piss-Poor Execution

As with everything, the devil is always in the detail.

When you boil all of these insights down to the lowest common denominator what you will find is that your ability to Capture Value really comes down to one simple test: Can you raise prices without losing clients or incurring resistance?

Pricing power is what separates the Googles of this world from the airlines. Plain and simple.

If you can go out today and raise your prices without fear and without losing a bunch of clients, then you've got a decent practice. If, like Dan, you have to cross your fingers, lose sleep, and pray to the pricing gods before you do it, then you do not have a good business.

Pricing power really comes down to Thiel's monopoly benchmark. If you own your market or have a service that is highly differentiated and cannot be duplicated by your competitors, then you control your market and can set prices accordingly. There are a few notable businesses that fall into this category—Apple, Disney, Google, Coca-Cola, SAP, DeBeers, Oracle, and a few others.

If 90 percent of what you do right now is undifferentiated (bookkeeping, tax returns, payroll, reconciliations, and so on) then you are going to struggle to create pricing power and Capture Value. Your job is to find enough Economic Value above and beyond the time and materials that go into providing those services, so that you can justify setting your price based on a percentage of the value that you create for your clients.

And for those of you who are convinced that it is impossible to command a premium price for the compliance work that you are currently doing, you may want to reconsider this mindset in light of what Nespresso has accomplished. As you well know, coffee beans are often referred to as a commodity. Let's take a closer look and examine whether that classification holds weight or not. Nespresso created a device that brews an individual serving using small capsules in the process (instead of loose beans). The Economic Value that they created in their device (which is simply a delivery mechanism) has allowed them to sell $19 worth of beans (the RRP for one kilogram of coffee beans) for around $137.

Their ability to Capture enormous Value, for a product like coffee, is proof that it can be done. But you must change your mindset and your approach to manifest this result in your practice.

At the end of the day, it's not going to be enough to simply Create Value for your clients. If you want to Price Value, you must find a way to Capture Value for yourself and use it to further invest in Creating even more Value for your clients in the future. If you miss this step, you are leaving money on the table, which means you may not have adequate funding in the future to invest in what is required to keep you afloat.

And just to be clear on this point before we move on, pricing power has nothing to do with your brand. One of the biggest mistakes and distractions you could make is to get caught up in your branding (i.e., what you call your firm), as opposed to focusing 100 percent of your resources and effort on Pricing Value.

If your brand is linked to Creating and Capturing Value, then we would expect to see a one-to-one relationship between brand strength and economic returns. This is in fact not borne out statistically. Your branding is in fact of little relevance to your ability to Capture Value and exert pricing power, yet so many accountants make the rookie mistake of placing far too much time and emphasis on it.

How to Capture More Value

So we have come to the conclusion that Capturing Value is often overlooked to the detriment of many businesses and accounting practices—Capturing Value is in fact far more important to the value of your firm than Creating Value.

But just how widespread is this problem and what can you do about it?

According to the research of Professor Stefan Michel, most companies spend the bulk of their time and attention on Creating Value, to the detriment of Capturing Value. In his words: "My work with more than 50 companies in dozens of countries has confirmed for me that businesses have spent far more time, money, and effort on value-creating innovations than on value-capturing ones—and that much can be gained by correcting the imbalance."[4]

In Pricing Value, both Creating Value and Capturing Value are important. Interestingly, 98 percent of your competitors are predominately focused on Creating Value only.

In good times (when there is little disruption or competition) you might be able to get away with just concentrating on Creating Value for a short time. However, when you fail to Capture Value in your practice, what that means is you are leaving money on the table, and the only way

---

[4] Professor Stefan, M. 2014. "Capture More Value," *Harvard Business Review*, October 2014, https://hbr.org/2014/10/capture-more-value

to future-proof your practice is to go after that money and find ways to Capture more Value. You can achieve that by changing your pricing mechanism (i.e., demand driven, value-based, auctioning, and so on), changing the payer, changing the carrier (i.e., bundling, all inclusive models), changing the timing, changing the segment, or changing the system.

Let's explore two key strategies to capture more value in the context of Pricing Value—segmentation and systems.

Segmentation

If you only have one price for a given service or solution in your accounting practice, you are pricing too high for some clients and too low for others. Each client will attribute a different level of value to a same or similar service. For example, charging $500 a month for a compliance-only service may be incredible value for a $10M company but far too expensive for a small limited business turning over under $50,000.

By pricing according to each client's willingness-to-pay, you can capture the maximum amount of revenue relative to the value you create (which of course drives your firm's value). Have a look at this visual representation of this concept (see Figure 6.2).[5]

What this diagram shows is that, in most cases, money that is currently being left on the table by having a fixed rate (i.e., areas shaded in white) can often be collected by you with little effort and very few additional costs—which means it often flows down directly to your bottom line as profit and cash flow.

Moving to differentiated pricing, which is based upon segmenting clients and then pricing each of them individually, has been shown to generate anywhere from 12 percent to 30 percent of lift in revenue (with virtually no incremental costs). That means those revenues could flow down to the bottom line and result in an increase of 50 percent or more in operating profit and cash flow, which is substantial.

---

[5] Alex, H. 2017. "How to Capture More Value With Price Segmentation." *CFO Newsletters*, July 6, 2017, http://ww2.cfo.com/strategy/2017/07/capture-value-price-segmentation/

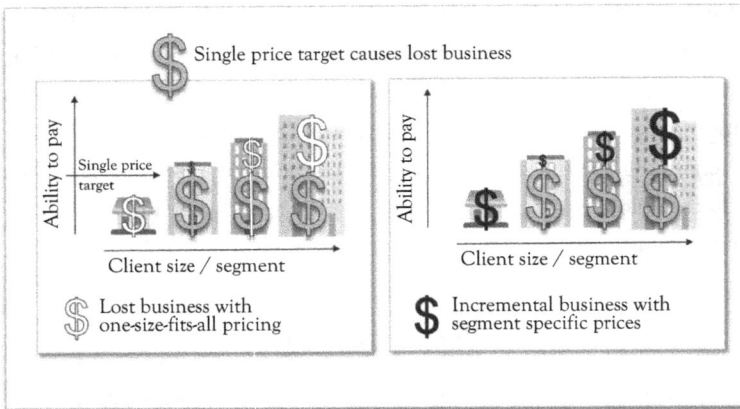

Figure 6.2 Pricing Per Your Client's Willingness to Pay Results in Higher Value Capture

In order to achieve meaningful and relevant segments to begin with, the best firms are using a combination of context, customer data, transactional data, and business judgment. There are several well-established statistical methods for analyzing your client history and identifying pricing segments based on the attributes of each sale. These elements tend to fall into four categories:

- Product/Service—examining the nature of what is being sold.
- Client—information about the industry, client size, end-use application, price sensitivity, and so on.
- Transaction—data related to the number of transactions and frequency.
- Delivery—how the product/service is delivered to each client.

Determining the best level of segmentation for your practice is a bit of a trial and error process. Too little granularity will lead to sub-optimization in pricing because you are still likely to be pricing far too broadly. Too much granularity can also lead to too many segments and confusion.

Statistically speaking, only 15–20 percent of your clients will be focused on price (the low segment). The majority (60 percent) are focused on content (the standard segment), and the remaining 15–20 percent prefer premium offerings (how the service is delivered).[6] What this means is that clients who fall into the low segment are typically more price conscious—they will often be willing to accept off-peak, lower benefits, more restrictions, lower quality, and less support for a better price. If you are dealing with a client who falls into this category, you might want to structure your packages so that they receive solutions to most of their pain points at the mid-price package, but they have the option to upgrade or downgrade depending on their priorities and price sensitivity.

With clients that fall into the standard category, spend particular time assessing which components of Economic Value go to content and which essentially relate to how the service is delivered. This does not mean that a standard client will not self-select to a premium price, but it does mean that they will be more focused on the value of the pain that is cured, and less so on the support they receive, and so on. This means they may select to do some of it themselves if they are reluctant to take up your highest price package. To entice them to take up higher price packages, consider options that assist them to collate their information, technology that makes getting data to you seamless/painless, and so on. They will often opt to pay more if you clearly make their life easier.

With premium clients, they want you to take the pain away and they will gladly pay you for the privilege of not having to worry about any of it. These are also the most likely to take up options such as concierge services, working with a specific practitioner, 24 hour turnaround, or audit insurance, and so on.

Systems

It is almost impossible to Capture Value masterfully and consistently while "winging it." There are far too many variables to consider and it pays huge dividends to enter into this process with a strong system or template for approaching each client to Capture Value.

---

[6] Frederiksen, L., E. Harr, and S. Montgomer. 2017. "Inside the Buyers Brain." Reston, VA, https://hingemarketing.com/wp-content/uploads/2016/03/Inside_The_Buyers_Brain_Webinar

Once you have segmented your clients, you must develop a strong template for presenting your prices in a manner that will give you the best chance of achieving the maximum value that your client is willing to pay. This will include decisions about how many choices to offer and how to present those in a way that maximizes the amount each client is willing to pay. It also includes some rigor around how you might employ options and behavioral rewards to slowly inch your client toward an engagement that will maximize the value you deliver to them and also capture significant value for your firm.

CHAPTER 7

C#5 Communicate Value

There are three key factors you must take into account when mastering the skill of Communicating Value:

- Certainty.
- Choice.
- Cure.

When Communicating Value, your client must have certainty, choice, and the cure, if you want them to decide. For all the reasons discussed in earlier chapters, achieving certainty is relatively straightforward once you have made the conscious decision to Price Value. However, the factors of choice and cure are a bit more elusive.

To that end, let's take a look at how to determine the optimal number of choices to give your client, why there is a right and a wrong way to pitch your solution, and finish up with some key tips to ensure your client believes you and is confident enough to say "yes." As you are about to discover, it's not enough for you to simply say that you can cure their pain. You must prove it to them beyond a shadow of a doubt, because if you don't, they simply won't decide.

Why Is Choice Crucial?

Choice is crucial for several reasons, the first being that it puts your client in control of the buying process. The second reason is even more fundamental because it is grounded in neuroscience AND it also goes to the essence of why you are Pricing Value in the first place: no two clients will place exactly the same value on any given service.

Choice can theoretically be achieved by offering a selection of fixed packages or a range of value-based prices. Unfortunately, only one of these approaches is fair to both you and your client. Let's examine why that is...

Imagine a situation where you stay back late at the office one night to work on the tax return of a client. Because it's quiet and everyone else has gone home, you've got two whole hours to get lots of work done with no interruptions. And for the sake of example, let's assume you spend one hour photocopying and collating the information for the client and the second hour developing a strategy you are sure will save him $34,000 from his tax bill this year. Now, what most of you are doing is billing the client as if the value from those two hours is equal—whether you do it in the form of an hourly or fixed rate. However, it's patently obvious that the value created, at least in the eyes of your client, is vastly different from the first to the second hour, isn't it?

Put simply, fixed packages are terrible for setting the price of your accounting services because they rarely allow enough choice, they fail to take into account the value created for your client, and they often do not allow you to Capture Value in any significant way.

But let's come back now to your need to offer options to quench the thirst your clients have for choice. The question that you should now be asking is: "How many options is ideal?"

Determining the Optimal Number of Options

As you take a leisurely stroll down the aisle of your nearest grocery store, it's easy for your eyes and your mind to feel overwhelmed among the 20 different choices of "must have" laundry detergents and kitchen counter cleaners. A supposedly quick, five-minute dash to the store to pick up cleaning products usually turns into a 25-minute ordeal simply because you are bombarded with 6 different brands and 16 different formulations of essentially the same thing. Perhaps not surprisingly, it takes time (and a lot of processing power) for your brain to figure out what's the best option. And thinking is not conducive to deciding.

So, why do retailers (and many other businesses) offer so many options? Is there any validity to the claim that "more choice equals greater sales"?

Unfortunately, businesses fall into the trap of thinking they need to offer more options in order to boost sales. Even though consumer behavior and neuromarketing studies have proven this theory to be patently incorrect, many fail to understand that offering an abundance of products or services does not guarantee more sales.

In fact, often an increase in choices causes an increase in buying complications, fatigue, and indecision. Recent research confirms that many companies are forfeiting sales by providing customers with far too many options.

To understand this phenomenon, a Columbia University and Stanford research team formulated a study to measure the relationship between the number of options offered and total sales. Outside a grocery store in Menlo Park, California, the team offered customers varying selections of exotic jams. Within a 48-hour period, 502 consumers were offered a variety of either six different flavored jams or 24.[1]

While displaying the 24 different flavors, only 0.03 percent of the prospective buyers pulled the trigger and made a purchase. However, when the variety of flavors was slashed to a manageable number like 6, 30 percent of consumers bought the jam.

Clearly, more options doesn't always equate to more purchases. Why is that?

The human brain is configured to favor expeditious decision-making. Remember, your brain consumes a lot of energy when it thinks, so it is hardwired to decide quickly without relying on the need to do a whole lot of thinking. Therefore, the introduction of too many choices will often create confusion, overwhelm, and a feeling of "needing to go away and think about it."

Surprisingly, your short-term memory is only capable of successfully processing information in small bite-sized chunks, preferably three to four at a time. So, it makes good financial sense to offer fewer varieties or options that can be quickly and easily digested!

So how does all of this apply to your accounting practice and the pricing options you offer to your clients?

---

[1] Iyengar, S.S., and M.R. Lepper. 2000. "When Choice is Demotivating: Can One Desire Too Much of a Good Thing?." *Journal of Personality and Social Psychology* 79, no. 6, pp. 995–1006. https://faculty.washington.edu/jdb/345/345%20 Articles/Iyengar%20%26%20Lepper%20(2000).pdf

It turns out that this research is also directly relevant to the number of pricing options you provide to your clients. Remember, while your clients desire choice, only three or four pieces of information can be processed at once by the part of their brain that decides.

Overloading them with too much information about your services and too many options/choices for the price will only delay the decision-making process and cause you to lose sales.

If you want to make it easier for your clients to say "yes," offering only a small handful of options is old-brain friendly. That is one of the reasons why many experts in pricing advocate offering three options. Later, in Chapter 9, we will examine a compelling reason (and some empirical evidence) why three is likely the optimal number of choices for Pricing Value.

Pitching the Right Way

As you are beginning to realize, humans find it almost impossible to think rationally about pricing. If anyone tries to tell you that you can win over a client with logic around pricing, they are incredibly naive. Unfortunately, the old brain doesn't respond to rational arguments.

Because of this, thoughts (either the client's or your own) about pricing are virtually useless in setting an effective strategy. Remember, your brain is hardwired to decide and act quickly, to keep you out of harm's way. Pricing may not make sense to the rational, thinking parts of your brain—and it doesn't have to in order for you to make decisions that are good for your practice and for your clients.

You have now arrived at the critical point in the Pricing Value model where you have the opportunity to paint a picture—to give them a clear visual (either in words or pictures) of how your solution will deliver the value they seek. It's the moment where you will begin to outline the Economic Value, your unique solution, the proposed pricing, requirements, responsibilities, timelines, and so on.

Please remember, at this stage your client has still not agreed to purchase, which means that this is not the time to go into great depth on every step you will take in the process. These sorts of details will cause them to think too much and it will interfere with or delay the decision making process.

First and foremost, it's imperative to Communicate Value face to face wherever possible. The reason for this is twofold. First, it allows you to deal with questions and objections quickly and get them out of the way. The second reason is even more fundamental—you must involve the client in the process. Involvement allows him/her to assess the options, prioritize, and decide. Failure to involve the client in the process is the single biggest reason why most attempts to Price Value fail miserably.

Michael learned this lesson the hard way. He used to invite clients and prospective clients to his accounting practice for a chat. Sometimes, just to keep it informal, he'd even pop out with them to the local coffee shop next door.

During the course of the meeting, he found himself delving into great detail about all the great services that he could offer them—tax planning, cash flow forecasting, corporate restructuring, business improvement advice, and so on. These little talks could go on for almost an hour without the client really ever getting a word in edgewise, let alone actually understanding most of what he said. It all sounded impressive, but since the majority of his clients weren't financially savvy, most had no idea what it all meant for them personally.

But inevitably at some point, the client would interject and ask, "How much is this all going to cost?"

Here's where everything went off the rails for Michael...

Since Michael had not used a systemized process to Comprehend, Create, and Capture Value for the client, panic would set in when asked about the price—he was put on the spot by his client and he didn't want to risk under quoting. So he did exactly what most of you are doing, and came up with this response, "I don't know, I need to go away and think about it."

And without knowing it, Michael inadvertently shot himself in the foot. He went away for a few days (or even a week), created a lengthy written proposal detailing all of the services and costs, and then sent it to them. More often than not, weeks would go by and Michael was left wondering why he never heard back, or worse, the client couldn't seem to make a decision.

Here's the most important point that you need to know about pitching—sending a quote/proposal without first Comprehending, Creating, and Capturing Value, and then Communicating that Value verbally (preferably face to face) is a fatal mistake, which is almost impossible to recover from. You cannot Price Value if you haven't completed each of those steps with your client.

Here's the reason for this. When you send your quote/proposal through the mail (snail mail or electronic), you lose control of the process and your client is also much more likely to be price conscious. It also means that your client was not at all involved in the actual process of setting the options and ranking the priorities for curing each of their pain points.

Think about it. Because your client is time-poor and the decision-making part of his or her brain is hasty and impatient, he or she will always skip directly to the section where you have noted the price, make a snap judgment about it being "expensive," and completely miss or overlook everything that you have written in the proposal.

In most cases, it's almost impossible to recover from a fatal mistake such as this because the client has already made a decision that your price is too high. And once they have made a decision, it is much harder to change their mind.

Wherever possible, you must Communicate Value face to face. Ideally, you must do it immediately after Comprehending, Creating, and Capturing Value. To give yourself the best chance of success, you must Price Value when the magnitude of your client's pain points is fresh in their mind and they can remember the Economic Value that you will provide with your solution.

Think back to our example in Chapter 1 of the person who is crawling across the desert in 104°F (40°C) heat, looking for water to stay alive. Ask yourself this vital question: "When is the value of your proposed solution the highest?"

If you let your client go away for a week to read the proposal at their leisure, is he or she likely to be more or less motivated to cure the pain you discussed today?

If you can see that your client is clearly in pain and needs help in some aspect of his or her business, it does not make sense to let them off the hook. If they walk away without committing to make changes in their business, the pain points will not magically fix themselves. Their cash flow or staff retention issues, and so on, will continue to be bad and prevent them from earning a decent living or growing. You are in fact doing them a huge disservice when you let them walk away without taking some sort of action.

If you have just spent an hour building up the depth of his or her thirst, their confidence and motivation to step into your solution is at its highest point right now. Therefore, now is the time when you should Communicate Value.

Some experts advocate that it is okay to go away after Comprehending, Creating, and Capturing Value to put together a proposal and then present it on another day to your client. That approach is incongruent with the scientific research on how the brain processes information and makes decisions. If the client in front of you is dying of thirst and you offer them a chance to go away, have a few glasses of water, and think about it, you are much more likely to lose the sale.

You must pitch your solution (i.e., Communicate Value) at the time when the depth of their thirst is the highest. Yes, it is acceptable to follow up with a written proposal for them to peruse later. But ideally you want to Communicate Value face to face (when their thirst is at its greatest) and get an indication from them which option they are leaning toward based on their priorities.

Codifying Value

Before you can even think of pitching to your client, you must first determine what price options you will offer and how you should codify those in a proposal or agreement. Because Pricing Value is an experience or feeling, not a mathematical formula, no one can give you a hard and fast template that will work every time with every client. However, there are some helpful guidelines and factors that you must take into account when codifying value.

First and foremost, the starting point is always the same—the answers that you received from your client back in Chapter 4—Comprehend Value. Based upon these answers, your assessment of Economic Value, your ability to deliver a unique solution that cannot easily be compared to your competitors, plus your client's price sensitivity (if any), you can begin to outline some pricing options.

It is crucial to remember that statistics indicate that only a small percentage of clients are actually price sensitive. As explained in the previous chapter, only 15–20 percent of your clients will be focused on price. The majority (60 percent) will be focused on content and/or value, and the remaining 15–20 percent prefer premium offerings.

Once the client has selected the option that suits him/her best, it should then be codified in a written agreement. The agreement should include:

- A clear picture of what the outcome looks like.
- Your unique claim/solution (that disqualifies your competitors).
- Investment required (pricing options and terms)—link directly to results.
- Timeline and milestones.
- Client responsibilities re: delivered inputs.
- Your responsibilities.
- Scope of work and other planning details.
- After action reviews and how frequently those will be conducted with the client.
- Updated engagement letter.

Does Your Client Believe You Can Cure Their Pain?

We explored in previous chapters how crucial it is to Comprehend, Create, and Capture Value. To date, a lot of time and attention has been invested by you to really understand what is important to your client. However, the integral role of communication should not be overlooked or underestimated. In fact, C#5 is just as crucial as the four preceding Cs because it ensures that all the hard work you have done so far doesn't go unnoticed by your client.

This is the step where you get to present, explain, and prove value.

Language is powerful. It holds the potential to move people to action or cause them to hesitate. It also includes both the words you say and how you say them. Let's explore a handful of powerful techniques you can employ to Communicate Value masterfully.

1. Be Up Front About Price

If you present your potential clients with a document that outlines the proposed engagement, goals, milestones, responsibilities of both parties, and so on, it is never a good idea to place the price on the final page. One of two things is likely to happen—(1) your potential client will be impatient, skip to the end to read the price, and you will lose the sale because they failed to Comprehend the Value, or (2) they will exhaust themselves mentally reading the entire document and the only thing they will remember at the end of it all will be the price.

Either way, you are likely to lose the sale. Burying the price at the end actually draws attention to the price, which makes your clients more likely to become price conscious.

Remember, according to neuroscience, the brain pays 100 percent attention at the beginning and end of every interaction.

If circumstances necessitate that you send the quote or a follow up in writing, you must:

- Position the cost of doing nothing, the Economic Value, and your unique, bespoke solution first.
- Next, outline your price options and the scope of the work.
- Ensure you conclude with a clear statement/picture of the Economic Value and unassailable proof that you can cure the key pain points.

It is imperative that the Economic Value, your unique solution, and proof are the things that your client sees first and last—thus, they will remember and pay attention to them. This sets the scene in their brain for them to prioritize the solving of key pain points and deflects their attention away from the proposed price. You should always quote the price options, scope of the work, timelines, and responsibilities, and so on in the body of the proposal as you now know that your client's brain will only be at 20 percent attentiveness when skimming this information.

This deliberate structure will leave your client squarely focused on value and proof, and not on the price.

2. Price Your Client Face to Face

For all of the reasons outlined earlier in this chapter, you should present your pricing options in a face-to-face meeting with your client. If face-to-face is not achievable, try Skype video or another electronic means to connect visually with your client. Remember, this is exactly where Michael made his fatal pricing mistake. While devastating, it is also completely avoidable as there are several ways to price your client face to face.

3. Link Directly to Results

When we covered C#3 Create Value, we introduced the concept of Economic Value. While some marketers talk about turning features into benefits, you already know that clients will only pay pennies for your features and benefits (i.e., glass of water exercise in Chapter 1), but they will pay any price for THE solution. The solution is derived from Economic Value. It is what makes your solution the only sane option, regardless of price.

You are no longer in the business of just pumping out tax returns or bookkeeping services. You must determine what the Economic Value is above and beyond the time and materials that go into delivering those services. When you describe the scope of the work you will be carrying out, it needs to specifically link back to the results/value that your client asked for.

Make no mistake, this point is crucial. If you do not directly link back to actual results/value, your client may not be able to see the value you have worked so hard with them to Comprehend, Create, and Capture.

4. Make It Impossible to Draw Price Comparisons

As you discovered earlier, clients base their perceived value (price) on reference points. If you're selling a service, most will look around and find another service to compare yours to. If that search uncovers that your competitors sell the exact same thing for $200, then this will impact their overall perception of the "right price" for the service.

If your solution is at the leading edge, highly specialized/relevant, or disruptive, there may be no clear price reference. In this instance, prospects are much more likely to accept the price you determine.

However, if your generic service is more expensive than the common reference points in your industry, you will need to take action to change the perception of the category or the uniqueness and value that your specific solution provides.

If you want to Price Value, you must either create a new category or deliver a solution that is so unique (highly specialized and relevant) that it cannot easily be duplicated by your competition. This is another reason why it is imperative to niche down. The more expertise you have in a particular niche, the greater the likelihood you immediately disqualify your competition. At this point in the process, you should be asking yourself, "What can I become the BEST in the world at?"

Even with routine compliance work—bookkeeping, tax returns, and so on—you can always uncover or create more Economic Value above and beyond the basic time and materials it takes to deliver the service. What can you do to go "above and beyond" in delivering your solution that makes what you do invaluable and irreplaceable to your client?

Think about factors such as timeliness of access to information to make better decisions about running the business, pre-emptive advice to avoid cash flow or working capital pain in the foreseeable future, turnaround time, support, training, workflow improvements (efficiencies), and so on. These need to form the core foundation of your message when you Communicate Value to your client.

Your goal is to create and communicate Economic Value so clearly that it is impossible for a client to compare you based on price to any other competitor. The whole point of doing this is to make price a non-issue and render your solution the only sane option.

CHAPTER 8

C#6 Convince

In the 1970s Corning Glass introduced an innovative product, safety glass. A young salesman with little experience joined the company and began working his way up through the sales department at a feverish pace. In very little time, this young man named Bill became the top-selling salesman of safety glass in North America. He stunned management with his rapid achievements and became known for refusing to use the standard templates and presentations that most of the other salesmen relied blindly upon.

At the national sales convention, he was given an award for his achievements and was asked by the president to share his secrets. Everyone seated in the room that night waited on the edge of their seats to discover just how this young man, with no prior sales experience, was able to outsell everyone.

To the president's invitation, Bill explained, "First of all, I commissioned some samples of safety glass cut into 6″ squares and I purchased a hammer and safety goggles. Rather than boring my audience with small talk, or building up my credibility, I would simply walk into the room, greet my prospect, and open with the question, 'Would you like to see a piece of glass that doesn't shatter?'"

And he never met a single one who turned him down.

In fact, they were all eager to take part in his little experiment and jumped at the chance to pull on the safety goggles, put the glass on the desk, and whack it with the hammer. They loved every minute of it and inevitably when they couldn't break it, they would take the goggles off, sit back in their chairs and exclaim, "Holy smoke, that's incredible!"

Then Bill would simply say, as he paused strategically and drew the adoring crowd in closer for more of his wisdom, "Given that you lose $x every day due to broken glass, how much of this unbreakable glass would you like?" And he'd pull out his order pad and start writing up the order.

Well, as you can imagine, Corning Glass was so impressed that they equipped all of their salespeople with goggles, hammers, and small sample sheets of glass. They sent them out and found that the average closing rate shot up by almost 29 percent.

How would your life and practice change if clients were drawn to you like a magnet and closing was just a formality that you no longer needed to dread?

Now granted, this specific strategy is ideally tailored to work for selling safety glass and it's not going to work (without some modifications) to get your clients excited to pay for your business solutions that are priced based on the value you can help them to create.

However, the salient point, and what you should take away from this example, is this: the top salesman never had to "close the sale," deal with objections at the 11th hour, or discount his price. From the outset, his presentation identified, quantified, and cured the #1 source of pain for his prospects. Plus he proved beyond a shadow of a doubt that it could do what he said it would.

That is why the sale was a "done deal" even before Bill pulled out his order pad—his pitch was old-brain friendly and did most of the heavy lifting for him. And that is the ultimate goal that you are now working toward in your client interactions (both before and after the initial sale).

Convince Is Not as Daunting as You Think

Convince is not just another step in the process of Pricing Value. Convince is imbued into every step of the Pricing Value Model.

If you uncover what is of value, gain leverage on your client, and execute each of the other five Cs masterfully, you should NOT have to work hard to close your clients (i.e., convince). If you have mastered everything else, Convince should be the easiest step to execute as you have set the entire interaction up perfectly for your client to be motivated and confident to help themselves by stepping into your solution immediately.

You should never view this process as needing to "learn how to sell" or "close." That implies that you need to "get your client to buy" by using tactics or strategies on them. The truth is, your client is in a lot of pain right now (or there is a huge chasm between where they are and where they need to get to). If they do nothing today, that pain is not going to magically go away. In fact, it may actually get worse. The best way you can help them is for you to show them the cost of continuing to ignore the problems and how easy it can be for them to step into your solution that cures them once and for all.

When you implement what you have learned so far, you pave the foundation to Convince them effortlessly and rapidly. Convince is not an afterthought or a tactic—it is interwoven into every other step of the Pricing Value system. By following the simple step-by-step Pricing Value system, you are essentially laying out the proverbial breadcrumbs for your clients to follow (like Hansel and Gretel in the children's story) to your unique solution. You are making it easy for them to help themselves to the solution.

Let's take a look at each of the steps that we have already covered in the Pricing Value model and examine how each contributes to putting your client in the best frame of mind to say "yes" without you needing to "work hard" to Convince them.

In the first two chapters you discovered the key to Pricing Value—knowing what is of value to each client and how to gain leverage on them. Having a powerful stable of relevant, probing, and insightful questions to Comprehend Value (i.e., draw out their pain points and vision for the future) allows you both to understand the magnitude of the problem/challenge and the cost of continuing to ignore it. This is where you build up the depth of his or her thirst and create substantial motivation for your client to take action to fix the problem. Clients who are in extreme pain (high cost/risk, life or death, and so on) will pay any price for the solution. They are also unlikely to put off making a decision or invent objections if their thirst has them crawling across the desert to your oasis.

You now also know how important it is to Control Your Fear in this process. Your level of confidence and focus is directly proportionate to the level of confidence and clarity your client will feel about working with you. If you are unsure about your own value, your client will mirror that doubt back to you. If you are afraid of change, your client will hesitate. If you are afraid to increase price, your client will focus on the number instead of the value. You also learned a powerful reframing process that you can repurpose and use when you need to diffuse and overcome objections (more about this later in the chapter).

Next, you discovered how to determine Economic Value as part of the process of Creating Value—the value your solution provides above and beyond the time and materials that went into producing it. By helping your client get crystal clear about the magnitude of the problems and value of the solutions, you intensify his or her desire to act now in order to solve them with you. We also discussed a few powerful but subtle techniques to influence your client's perception of value, and these are invaluable to framing up the environment to lead them to a "yes." These techniques have little to do with the actual numerical price but everything to do with how your client views and assesses value. Clients who perceive great value (tangible or intangible) are unlikely to need a lot of convincing.

Unfortunately, it's not enough to diagnose pain, create Economic Value, and present your unique claim(s) as the best cure—you must also prove it to your clients if you want them to decide. Remember, if your prospect or client doesn't believe that it will work, he or she will not decide or they will walk away. When your client believes beyond a shadow of a doubt that you can cure their pain, your job to Convince becomes infinitely easier. The vast majority of your competitors will make the fatal mistake of outlining their new valued-added packages and assuming that the audience will take their word for it. Mastering the art of communicating proof will put you ahead of 95 percent of your competitors.

We also explored the specific techniques that you can use to Capture Value in the prices that you offer. By involving your client in the process of setting those prices and examining their own priorities, you have already received their initial agreement to purchase. When your client engages in the process of agreeing to or adjusting priorities, they have already made the decision at a deeply unconscious level to engage you. Every single "yes" is a small step toward a "yes" for the overall engagement. And from a behavioral psychology point of view, clients who have already said yes to various components along the way are less likely to object or need time to decide. You also learned a few additional techniques such as managing the number of options you give, bundling, and context—all of these help to make it easier for your client to decide, which means you don't have to work hard to try to Convince them.

Finally, you gained clarity on the key points that you need to Communicate Value and the level of proof required to make your package options old-brain friendly. You also learned how invaluable it is to pitch the options and prices to your clients face to face and how you can use segmentation to help structure your pricing packages so they are more relevant and persuasive.

In the next chapter, you will learn that it is not enough to have three packages—that there is an art and a science behind how you must structure your packages to make it easier for your clients to choose your premium offering.

The entire Pricing Value model has been developed with the concept of Convince woven into each and every component. Just like the breadcrumbs used by Hansel and Gretel, you are learning how to make it easier for your clients to see the obvious value of working with you and to be confident and motivated to say "yes" without having to do a whole lot of thinking (which can cause overwhelm and indecisiveness).

With Pricing Value, your primary job is to make your message old-brain friendly—this means you are pacing your client to feel comfortable and confident to say "yes" and you are also drawing out and pre-empting the common objections clients have as early in the process as possible.

Why Is It Crucial to Pre-empt Objections?

First and foremost, objections are not necessarily a bad thing so there is no need to fear them. Getting an objection does not mean your prospect is going to say "no," but it does mean that you have missed something important along the way that would have made it easier for them to say "yes" immediately. The objection is merely an opportunity for you to correct your oversight.

Prospects only tend to object when they are interested in saying "yes" but they still see obstacles/impediments to committing and paying you the money. It is impossible to prevent all obstacles/impediments, so there

is no point worrying about that. The most productive thing you can do
to make this step easier on you is:

- Put sufficient structure and systems in place during each
  interaction so you can identify, draw out, and diffuse
  objections early on in the process.
- Learn how to eliminate/diffuse the objection if and when one
  does come up.

Getting your process and mindset right is imperative because the
worst time for an objection to come out of the woodwork (especially one
that you are not expecting or prepared for) is at the end of the process
when your client is trying to decide. If possible, you must identify all
potential impediments early on in the process (by being meticulous with
your questions and your system) so you can ensure that your unique solution, claim, and proof specifically address and extinguish all objections.
You accomplish this when you are trying to establish the pain points and
the Economic Value component by asking questions such as "What is
the biggest reason that has held you back from finding a solution to this
problem?" Or "If you were going to decide right now, today, what would
be the most important factor to influence you?"

In a nutshell, you should not present your solution and pricing
options if you are not crystal clear what potential objections your client
might raise. Having a system is vital because it gives you greater control
over the interaction. It ensures that you Convince at each step of the way
and tease out all impediments to your client making a decision before you
present your pricing.

Dealing with potential objections up front (early in the process)
means that when time comes for your client to decide, the momentum
is in your favor. Having an objection (or multiple objections) arise at the
very end slows the momentum down and shifts your client into thinking
mode. When this happens, your client is going to delay making a decision
and will often need time to go away and think about it.

So it's important to remember that an objection is not a bad thing.
If a potential client gives you an objection after you have presented
your pricing, it means they want to buy but you still need to remove an

impediment. It also means that you need to take note of what happened, and adjust your process to ensure that you draw out all objections earlier in your next meeting with a potential client.

Practice makes perfect.

Combating Common Objections

Let's take a look at a few tested and proven strategies that you can use to diffuse the most common objections if and when they arise:

- Doubt/trust—"How do I know this will work for me? Or how do I know you have the right experience to help me?"
- Complacency—"She'll be right, mate!"
- Price sensitivity.
- Politics—prior commitments to other vendors or requiring sign off by other key decision-makers who are currently not at the table.
- Timing—"I'm too busy right now."

Doubt is one of the easiest objections to combat. When a potential client has doubt, it means they are not yet convinced it is safe to trust and work with you. Now most of your competitors will make the rookie mistake of trying to assert their own personal credibility or competence by referring to their awards, certifications, and so on. This is one of the least persuasive methods.

By far the easiest and most effective way to overcome doubt is by introducing a customer testimonial that specifically addresses the key pain point(s) that your client has. From a neuroscientific point of view, it's the most persuasive form of proof and it's powerful because "if you say it, it means one thing but if a client says it in their own words, it means everything to your prospect."

Complacency cannot exist when the cost of continuing to ignore the problem is very high. The brain is hardwired to keep you safe and it responds to high contrast. If your client is complacent, what it means is that they do not yet see enough contrast between doing nothing, acquiring your solution, or choosing a competitor. This means you need to go back and ensure they fully understand what it costs them right now to put off making a decision. And if they still need a bit more incentive, it is advisable to reiterate the net gain other clients (exactly like them) received by taking action with you.

Price sensitivity simply comes down to not establishing enough Economic Value above and beyond the cost of time and materials in your solution. You must present a solution that is unique and so differentiated that it immediately disqualifies your competition and price becomes a non-issue. There are two ways to tackle this. If you have correctly presented your client with three pricing options, you can focus their attention on the pain points identified and their priorities relative to curing each of those. Put the focus on their priorities and ask which pain point cure can be deferred until a later date. Once that item has been removed, retest the adjusted prices.

The second way to tackle a price objection is to go back to the underlying value of each of the key pain points that you identified. You must get agreement from the client that these are correct and point out the daily, weekly, or monthly cost to them of continuing to ignore the problem. Next, you can contrast this with the unique, bespoke solution you are proposing. It is important to note that your solution must be unique. If what you are offering looks/sounds like something they can get from another accountant down the street, it is going to be very tough to overcome a price objection. If you want to avoid this objection altogether, you cannot continue to offer undifferentiated services.

If a prospective client brings up an objection that relates to politics (not having the economic buyer or key decision-makers at the table or having prior commitments to other vendors), you have not done your homework properly. These types of objections should never come up at the pricing stage as they should be uncovered and dealt with by you early on in the process. It never makes sense to devise solutions and pitch pricing if you have no chance of winning business because the economic buyer and/or decision-makers are not present. You cannot usually overcome an objection like this late in the process—for the most part, it means you have either completely wasted your time and you must start again from the beginning once you have removed all the impediments. Do not attempt to Price Value unless ALL the right parties are at the table. It is quite often easy to identify the key decision makers as you can simply ask the question "if we were going to go ahead today and decide to work together, are all the individuals who have a say/vote present for this discussion we are having right now?" The economic buyer is sometimes a bit more elusive. According to Alan Weiss, there are three simple questions that you can use to uncover who is the economic buyer:[1]

1. Is there anyone else that needs to be involved in the approval process? (If so, then you must go and see that person).
2. Do you have the budgetary authority to fund this project/proposal?
3. If you and I were to shake hands and agree to do business today, could I commence tomorrow?

Timing is a lame excuse and a red herring. If time management is an issue today, you can guarantee it will still be an issue down the road—in six or 12 months. A wise person once said, "There is always enough time to do everything that is worth doing." The truth is, it never comes down to time; it's always an issue of priorities. Your client is either motivated to act or they are not.

For example, if your tradesman client is using lack of time as an excuse, you may want to ask, "So every plumber has the exact same number of hours in his or her day. What do you think it is that separates you from the successful ones who have made the decision to act?" And then follow up with, "What will it cost you if you go another six months like this, and don't make X a priority?" If you have done your homework properly, you should be able to reiterate the exact cost they incur each day/week/month by not taking action.

The other crucial point to note is that a client who uses time as an excuse usually does not value their own time. This is the most dangerous type of client to have because it means they will not make good choices (their priorities are not straight) and they will also not value your time. You need to think long and hard when you encounter this sort of objection

---

[1] Weiss, A., 2002. *101 Questions for Any Sale Situation You Will Ever Face*, 5. https://alanweiss.com/styles/pdf/101%20Questions%20from%20Alan.pdf

because this may not be the type of client that you want to attract. People who do not value their own time will think nothing of wasting yours.

Could a Bit of Broken Glass Make You More Convincing?

Surprisingly, the dilemma you face right now in your practice has a whole lot more in common with Bill and his story about broken glass than you might think. You and your clients say "yes" to things every single day based on survival instinct, emotion, and messages that are old-brain friendly. You don't need to attend a sales training course with high pressure tactics designed to help you "close the deal."

You just need a simple system to follow that helps you to identify, quantify, and cure the #1 source of pain for your prospects, plus prove beyond a shadow of a doubt that you can do what you say that you will. Once your client is aware of the depth of their thirst, they will become motivated to find a way to quench it. Your job is to show them how your drink of water will quench that thirst and give them enough proof so that they believe you can do it.

CHAPTER 9

Psychology and Science of Value

Do you remember the character Tyler Durden, played by Brad Pitt in the movie *Fight Club*? In the film, he gave an epic speech on the rules for fight club—one that has become legendary and helped the film to garner a cult-like following.

For those of you who have not yet seen the show, the first rule of fight club is pretty simple and memorable—you do not talk about fight club. Ironically, the second and third rules of fight club are also equally uncomplicated and unforgettable... you do not talk about fight club.

Now, strangely enough, this crazy, confronting, and unforgettable address contains a simple, poignant, and powerful nugget of gold that will literally transform your pricing strategy and revolutionize the way you run your practice.

Let's face it, like fight club, pricing is a volatile topic because pricing inspires very strong emotional reactions. There's a reason for this—your brain's response to pricing is hardwired. When you see something that you perceive is overpriced, it triggers a response deep within you and you will react almost immediately—without thinking—you just innately know that "it's not good value."

Pricing can trigger a whole range of persuasive, powerful, and primitive feelings: envy, anger, lust, disgust, loathing, frustration, regret, and even pleasure. It's a potent potion. Prices are like pouring gasoline onto the fire of your most sensitive emotional responses.

In fact, nothing has the potential to push your buttons like pricing—which is why a guy like Martin Shkreli was able to push the pricing buttons of thousands of people. You might remember that Shkreli is the guy who bought a $9,000 bottle of wine, and tweeted a photo of the label to boast about it to his followers.

And if that doesn't ring a bell, more famously, he was the CEO of Turing Pharmaceuticals. In 2015, his company raised the price of a life-saving, anti-parasitic drug from $USD18 to $USD750 per tablet overnight. What that meant was many pregnant women who had come into contact with toxoplasmosis, or HIV and cancer patients with compromised immune systems, were at significant risk because they could not afford the drug they needed to stay alive. It would be an understatement to say he got slammed on social media the next day by the World Health Organization, Hillary Clinton and others because, as you would expect, thousands of people had some pretty strong emotional reactions to his pricing decision.

Perhaps not surprisingly, the opposite is also true…

When you see a mountain of tealights in IKEA marked with "100 pack $3.99," a 2 for 1 travel offer to your favorite destination, or an all you can eat seafood buffet on the strip in Las Vegas…there is only one possible response. "OMG that's insane. I need to snap it up right now because it's just too good to pass up."

You're probably smiling right now because you know pricing is very emotional. It's not a conscious decision to grab those tealights, book that vacation, or eat yourself into a frenzy at the buffet…but a primitive, innate, animal response to very deliberate and clever pricing signals.

To be fair, most of the time your response to pricing is absurdly complicated, illogical, tangled, and a bit narcissistic. Let's be honest, pricing is a minefield and you need to find some proven ways to circumnavigate it safely in your practice, without getting yourself blown up (or beaten up) in the process!

The First Rule of Pricing Value

The first rule of Pricing Value is that you don't talk about pricing.

While it's tempting to talk to your clients and potential clients about price, it's not your clients' job to set YOUR prices. No doubt they will definitely have strong opinions that they will be keen to share with you, but for the most part you CANNOT base your pricing strategy on them.

Here's why…

It is almost impossible to predict how your client will react to a particular price (or several pricing options) by simply asking them. To be fair, your client has no idea how they will react until they are actually put in the position of having to decide and buy.

There's only one proven and reliable way to find out what clients think about your price(s), and that is to sell them things.

Neuroscience and behavioral psychology have both verified that perceptions about price are fickle and deceiving—you can only get meaningful and dependable data when a decision is actually made (yes or no) and that can only take place in the heat of the moment when your client is making comparisons in their mind and choosing. In the absence of a real decision, you merely have speculation and hypothesis. Neither are solid enough for you to bet your practice on.

You see, meaningful perception of price is only possible when a real live comparison can be made to something else. When that comparison is made via subtle and sometimes undetectable, subconscious means, perceptions can actually be swayed or altered in your favor. And the only way to measure the impact of all these perceptions is of course by assessing how it changes the actual decision.

Take for example the old retailing adage, "What's the best way to sell a $2,000 watch? That's easy, merchandise it next to a $15,000 watch!" This phenomenon actually has a name—it's called anchoring.

In the 1970s, Tversky and Kahneman hypothesized that casually suggesting an initial figure to a test subject would cause them to use that figure as a starting point for estimating unknown quantities.

In their research, subjects were informally given the number 65 in conversation and then later asked to estimate the percentage of African nations that were members of the UN. The average response to their question was 45 percent.[1]

They then repeated the study with a second group but salted them with the number 10 up front. The average response of the second group to the exact same question was 25 percent. The correct answer to the question was 23 percent, which means the group that was primed with the number 65 estimated nearly twice the correct answer. Whereas the group casually predisposed to the number 10 estimated a much lower percentage.

---

[1] Tversky, A., and D. Kahneman. September 27, 1974. "Judgment Under Uncertainty: Heuristics and Biases." *Science* (New Series) 185, no. 4157, pp. 1124–31.

Unfortunately, all too often accountants make the fatal mistake of trying to discuss pricing with their clients. It's not your client's job to set your prices. It's your job to Comprehend, Create, and Capture Value. Once you have done that, you can confidently Communicate Value to your clients and then wait to see what their decision is. Only a yes or no answer to a real life scenario can give you the information you need to assess your prices.

And you now know that even their answer can be unconsciously manipulated simply by priming your client up front with the total Economic Value of your solution or your top-end advisory price. It's the professional services practice equivalent of merchandizing your packages next to the $15,000 watch.

The Second Rule of Pricing Value

The second rule is that you don't think about pricing.

As you are beginning to discover, humans find it almost impossible to think rationally about pricing. Because of this, your thoughts (and of course your client's thoughts) are virtually useless to you in setting your prices.

Remember, the part of your brain that decides makes decisions within milliseconds of seeing visual cues. This part of your brain reacts almost immediately based on visual cues and survival instincts and it doesn't rely on the slower parts of your brain to make decisions. Your brain is hardwired to decide and act very quickly, with minimal involvement from other parts of your brain.

Pricing Value may not make sense to the rational, thinking parts of your brain—and it doesn't have to in order for you to make decisions that are good for your practice and your clients.

Take for instance the example of Turing Pharmaceuticals. When the CEO raised the price of Daraprim from $USD18 to $USD750, they could have sustained a 98.1 percent drop in sales—and still made more money.

Similarly, when The Times introduced a paywall to the online version of their newspaper, the number of eyeballs on their digital service dropped by 98.7 percent (from 22 m down to only 300,000). Yet, the move to a paid service was still a huge financial success, even though the drop in the number of eyeballs was staggering. And if you think about it, the whole move was probably pretty daunting to the management team who took the leap of faith and made the decision anyway.

Perhaps not surprisingly, the paradigm shifts and changes that you need to make in your practice right now in order to grow safely and Capture more Value might be hard to make sense of rationally.

That is why it is vital to NOT over think Pricing Value.

There are thousands of interesting and valuable studies that have been published on pricing strategy and methodology. Your job is to digest those insights, apply them to your practice, and test them with real customers. Don't fall into the trap of over thinking it or prejudging what you think MIGHT happen.

When it comes to Pricing Value, over thinking is the quickest path to failure. Your thoughts are your worst enemy when it comes to pricing.

The best strategy for you is to learn from the leading research that has been done on this important topic and see for yourself how this changes the results you're getting in your practice. Over thinking is the enemy of Pricing Value. Like it or not, both you and your customer make decisions based on survival instincts and emotions, not rational thought. No amount of logic or rational argument can rescue a bad pricing decision. Your offer either Communicates Value, gives you leverage, and is old-brain friendly, or it isn't.

The Third Rule of Pricing Value

And that brings us to the third rule, which is you don't guess about pricing.

The only reliable and accurate way to make sense of all the pricing research and strategies is to implement, test, and measure. And this is a crucial point to note because many accounting professionals have fallen into the trap of implementing one or two strategies (for instance bundling or offering three pricing packages) only to find out that it failed miserably with their clients. It begs the question—are the research studies incorrect or is it possible that the strategies simply were not executed properly by the accountants who tried to apply them?

In the hands of an amateur, even a simple Bic lighter can be deadly...

Take for instance the notion of decoy pricing, or as some like to refer to it, the Magic of Three. Many are quick to jump on the bandwagon of this strategy without first gaining a strong fundamental understanding of why three options are said to "charm the old brain" and HOW the plans need to be structured in order to maximize sales. In fact, the sound bite "Magic of Three" branding does a huge disservice to this valuable body of research because it suggests, at least unconsciously, that just having three options will guarantee more sales.

However, as with most things, the devil is in the detail. And as you are about to discover, the real magic lies in how options are processed and acted upon by the brain and in the specific steps that you must take when structuring your packages if you want more of your potential clients to potentially choose your highest priced option.

Back in the 1980s, Joel Huber and Christopher Puto conducted some classic pricing experiments with university students as subjects. They wanted to find out how college students bought beer (and other stuff) and what the implications might be for consumer marketing in general.[2]

Surprisingly, the results of their experiments are still relevant today. Huber and Puto started out by offering their subjects two types of beer—cheap and expensive. Pretty straightforward, right?

Seventy percent chose the more expensive beer which was unexpected. After all, remember, we are talking about university students and most would assume that they are pretty price conscious. This nuance is crucial for you as an accountant—especially if you currently assume that all of your clients are price conscious. That is your belief, but it may or may not be fact. In order to establish it as fact, you would need to test and measure this hypothesis with your existing clients.

Next, they added a decoy—another cheap beer. Surprisingly, none of the students chose this new cheap beer, but its presence on the shelf distorted the entire market, pulling the center of pricing gravity downwards, and along with it, of course, sales declined.

---

[2] Huber, J., J.W. Payne, and C. Puto. June 1982. "Adding Asymmetrically Dominated Alternatives: Violations of Regularity and the Similarity Hypothesis." *Journal of Consumer Research* 9, no. 1, pp. 90–98.

Finally, they introduced an ultra premium beer which had the exact opposite effect—skewing the entire market upwards, and significantly boosting sales. The lesson from all of this was obvious and we still see it being confirmed by more recent research and applied almost everywhere. The 'Good, Better, Best' pricing strategy is alive and well for sales of everything from accounting software, to telephones, computers, health insurance, and many other products/services.

And of course many of you already know that this research was updated and modernized again by behavioral economist Dan Ariely.[3]

Ariely was intrigued by a puzzling set of options offered to prospective subscribers of Economist magazine: (1) access to all web content for $59, (2) a subscription to the print edition for $125, or (3) a combined print and web subscription, also for $125 (see Figure 9.1).

On the surface, this three-tiered offering might seem a bit odd. You may be wondering:

- Why bother with three offerings?
- Who in their right mind would choose option 2?
- Why not just say that the print subscription also includes access to the web version and eliminate the second option altogether?

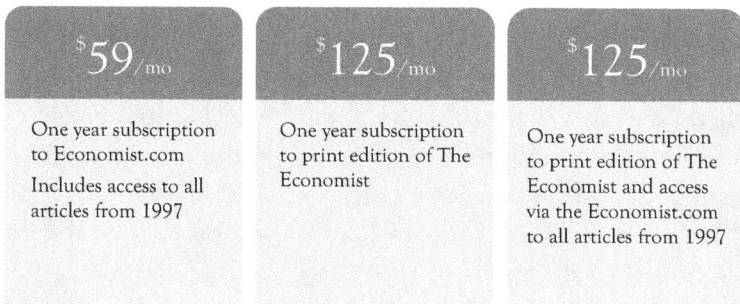

$59/mo
One year subscription to Economist.com
Includes access to all articles from 1997

$125/mo
One year subscription to print edition of The Economist

$125/mo
One year subscription to print edition of The Economist and access via the Economist.com to all articles from 1997

Figure 9.1 Testing the Good, Better, Best Strategy with Magazine Subscriptions

---

[3] Ariely, D. 2010. *Predictably Irrational.* New York, NY: HarperCollins Publishers.

Ariely decided to undertake some research and discovered something intriguing when he surveyed 100 students about which option they preferred. Very predictably, no one chose the print subscription alone (option 2). Eighty-four percent opted for the highest priced (the combination deal), and 16 percent for the web subscription only.

So it begs the question, if nobody chose the middle option, why offer it?

He repeated the poll with another 100 students—but this time, he removed the unpopular print-only alternative (option 2). And since no one chose it in the first instance, what difference could removing it possibly make?

Here's where his research gets interesting for you...

The second time around, 32 percent opted for the print and online subscription, while 68 percent preferred to go web-only. This seemingly unimportant change triggered a mammoth drop in sales of 30 percent—which is why this research is worth paying attention to.

However, it's essential to note that several decades worth of pricing research does not prove that offering three price options automatically guarantees an increase in sales or that most will choose your premium offering. If you jump to the conclusion that the "Magic of 3" is predicated solely on the number of options offered, you will have missed the point completely.

The first important point of distinction to note is this—searching for one perfect price is always exponentially less effective than offering a small range of prices. The range satisfies the crucial old brain driver of choice and the research has proven that if designed correctly, 3 is the optimal choice. Remember, choice equals safety to the brain because it means that your customer is in control of which solutions they acquire and when. Simply put, when your client feels safe, you will sell more.

The second most significant implication from four decades of pricing research goes to the notion of HOW you go about determining what the range of prices should be. As Dan Airely and others have proven, it is possible to reduce sales if the center of pricing gravity is too heavily skewed toward your lowest priced option.

To explain this in more depth, let's come back and take a deeper look at what you can learn from Ariely's research.

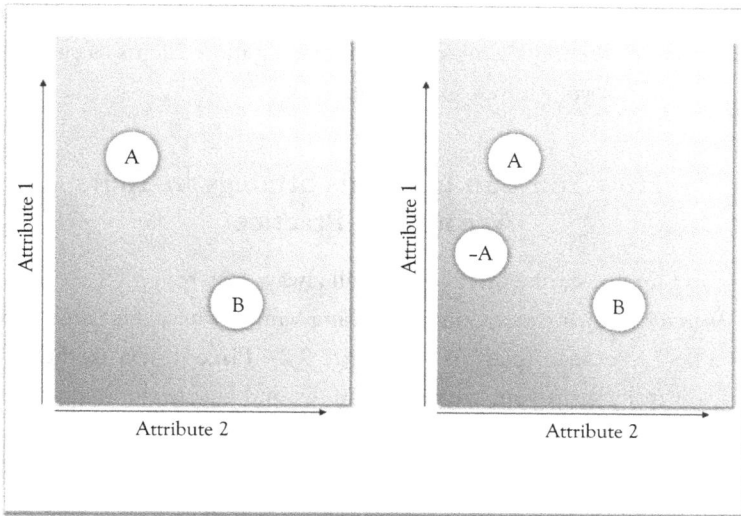

Figure 9.2 A Visual Depiction of Decoy Pricing

It appears as though the presence of the clearly inferior option (that is, the decoy—print-only option) altered the decision process by making the combined web and print subscription (option 3) seem like a much better deal. And Mr. Ariely has detected the same effect also applies in a range of other situations, including travel and perceptions of physical attractiveness, and so on.

So it appears as though the middle option (option 2) wasn't useless at all, but rather it helped people make a choice to buy the more expensive package, which then appeared to have more value. And this research also highlights the fact that sometimes people have trouble comparing different options, but if two of the options given are similar, but one clearly has more value, it makes it much easier for us to decide.

Here is a simple graph (Figure 9.2) that illustrates (in a very basic way) what happens when you introduce one option that is very similar (but still inferior) to your highest priced product or service.

So if you currently have two options for delivering a given service (say a tax return) in your practice—A which is top of the range with lots of Economic Value and B which is of lower value—it makes good financial sense to add a slightly worse option that is similar to A (call it A-).

The addition of A- makes it easier for your clients to see that A is clearly better than A-, hence you are subtly influencing more clients to choose A overall, and not your lowest priced option B.

How You Can Use This Strategy in Your Accounting Practice

First and foremost, one price option will always be wrong.

When Capturing and Communicating Value with a client, create and test a decoy package (plan A- per Figure 9.2). Place it next to the offer that you really want your clients to choose, and ensure the value differential (i.e., overall Economic Value) is very obvious and clear. You need to structure the three options so that it's a no-brainer for them to choose your A solution.

If you do not communicate very clearly that your premium package is obviously the best value, your offer will not be "old-brain friendly" which means your clients will struggle to decide and you risk losing 30–50 percent in revenue.

It is important to note that decoy pricing will not necessarily cause the majority to choose your A solution. And in fact, they do not need to in most cases for your firm to be much better off than before you started Pricing Value. However, the effective implementation of decoy pricing can have a significant impact on how many choose your premium offering and the overall increase in revenue across the board.

Remember, your clients can't tell you what they think about your value-based pricing, because they don't think about it...they feel it. You can't afford to keep guessing or over thinking your strategy, because pricing decisions are never made with the logical, thinking parts of the brain.

Price is the crudest, yet most subtle and persuasive message that you can send about your solution, so it's definitely worth investing your time to make it old-brain friendly. And in the end, the only way to do that is to take on board all of the research behind Pricing Value, apply it to your accounting services, Communicate Value to your clients, and measure the impact the changes have on sales and your bottom line.

PART II

Implementing Pricing Value

Part I of this book is dedicated to the core principles, psychology, and science behind Pricing Value. The balance of this book is dedicated to helping you take what you have learned and begin the process of implementing it in your practice using a systematic approach.

CHAPTER 10

Preparing for the Move to Pricing Value

Reading this book may have ignited a fire within your belly. You've probably been taking notes, sketching out your plans, and counting the benefits Pricing Value will bring to your practice. You may even feel like you're ready to jump in and start the ball rolling. But before you do, it makes good commercial sense to press the Pause button. Pricing Value in an ad hoc or haphazard fashion is actually potentially dangerous. To maximize the benefits for your firm and your clients, you must first embrace the complete philosophy behind Pricing Value.

Remember—Pricing Value requires a 180 degree turn in direction—both within you and in your practice. You'll be overhauling the way you approach and engage with your clients, how you communicate with them, the manner in which you price your solutions, and the method you use to Create and Capture Value. That is why it's imperative that you prepare your firm before taking this radical step.

Here is an example that will help you put the gravity of this into perspective…

After working his way up to the position of partner at Grant Thornton and creating a multi-million-dollar practice in the mining sector, Andrew decided for lifestyle reasons to go out on his own and create an independent practice. He dreamed of delivering great work for his clients but leaving the politics and headaches of a larger firm behind.

Andrew's practice grew rapidly. For two years in a row, it grew by 40 percent per annum—he went from grossing $800,000 to over $1.5m. While this enviable growth allowed him to expand his team, it also exposed certain bottlenecks and deficiencies in his practice. It eventually reached the point where he could no longer hide those flaws by simply working harder, and putting in longer days.

Andrew took a deliberate step back from his practice to gain some much needed perspective on his dilemma. This time away allowed him to clarify his vision for his practice and he was able to map out some initial steps he thought he needed to take in order to bring his vision into effect. Like many of you who are at the beginning of the journey to transform your practice, Andrew had an expectation that his team would have to work harder and more efficiently in order to achieve the firm's goal of growth. To his dismay, he discovered that many of his staff disagreed with his direction. Some chose to leave his team, inspiring others to follow. Within a relatively short period of time, he was forced to replace almost every single team member.

Truth be told, it was a really tricky time for Andrew because while he was busy recruiting and getting his new team up to speed, he also kept acquiring new clients. The challenge of training new employees while also needing to meet his clients' expectations, created even more difficulties for him. The deficiencies in his practice seemed to multiply and he soon found himself between a rock and a hard place. Both he and his team couldn't possibly work any harder and he soon began to regret his decision to leave Grant Thornton and start his own practice.

Around the time he officially hit rock bottom, Andrew did what most of you will instinctively do, and he took a stab at measuring the efficiency of his practice. He divided the money his firm billed each month by the number of working hours available.

$$\text{Practice Efficiency} = \frac{\text{Amount billed per month}}{\text{Number of billable hours per month}}$$

He punched the figures into his calculator, and pressed the Equals button. And as you might expect, Andrew recoiled in shock when he read the result. "Surely there must be a mistake," he thought? He doubled checked his numbers, and re-entered them. Unfortunately, the same figure appeared: $34.86. Basically, for every hour his team worked, they only generated a meager $34.86. And as you can well imagine, it wasn't enough to cover wages, let alone rent and other fixed expenses.

No wonder his cash flow—not to mention his confidence—had been flushed down the toilet!

As brutal as it was, this simple exercise (which most of you will probably do) clarified the issue in Andrew's mind. It caused him to conclude that he could no longer ignore his problems—the cost was too great. While this seemingly innocuous exercise gave him the motivation he needed to fix things, it also inadvertently sent him down the incorrect path toward focusing on efficiency in his practice. And that wrong turn was actually far more destructive than you or he could ever imagine.

You see, at this juncture, Andrew found himself in a classic Catch-22 situation. Even if he lifted his revenue by implementing Pricing Value, his team could not keep pace with the volume of client work coming through the door. And as for the idea of freeing up more capacity to Create Value for each client—forget it!

Andrew wanted to turn his practice around quickly by implementing Pricing Value. But before each team member could deliver the kind of value his big vision demanded, Andrew sensed that they needed to carve out more time to Comprehend and Create Value. What Andrew didn't realize was that this single-minded focus—on time and efficiency—would ironically take him further away from his goal.

Andrew was correct in coming to the conclusion that the move to Pricing Value required a fundamental shift in the way that he was currently operating his entire practice. To begin, he needed to build a strong foundation. This meant addressing his business systems, and streamlining practice workflows. Yes, he needed to free up capacity so that his team members could focus on Comprehending, Creating, and Communicating Value. However, that focus on time meant that he got caught up in the outdated notion he needed to track time and measure efficiencies. Unfortunately, neither of these two things (time and productivity) were of any value to his clients.

What he didn't realize is that this inward focus on his own operations didn't help Create Value for his clients and any gains that he might have made in profitability, wouldn't Capture Value for his firm. In the words of Peter Theil and Warren Buffet (explored in Chapter 6), none of these efficiencies were going to "stick to his ribs."

Standardize, Automate, and Simplify

Parts of Andrew's story will probably resonate with you because you probably face similar challenges right now in your own practice. Perhaps it might even feel a bit overwhelming? Wouldn't it be nice if you could just grab a proposal app to re-price each client and a timesheet app to measure how long your team works on each service? It sounds so easy, so clean—and yet, so potentially disastrous.

Remember: you don't have a pricing problem. You have a massive value discrepancy and you need to ensure that your practice is structured and streamlined to support the new way of doing business (i.e., Pricing Value) with your clients. The emphasis needs to be on the value you create for your clients and capture for your firm, not on the money or time you save by tightening your internal cost structures.

As you may have already discovered, small business clients are becoming increasingly savvy about what technology can and cannot do to boost results and help them grow. Due to changes in the way that they research and approach doing business with you, they are far less prepared to pay a premium for routine or compliance work because they know technology exists to automate many time-consuming and mundane tasks. In the past, these technologies were a threat because your billings were based on the time it took to complete each task. In fact, you were disincentivized to implement them because it meant your total revenue would decrease.

However, if you want to Price Value, you must master these new technologies before your clients hear about them. There are two important reasons for this. The first is you must free up capacity in order to create and deliver unique, relevant, and powerful solutions that cannot easily be duplicated by your competition. To do this, you must identify and implement better internal practices within your firm. If you fail to do this properly up front, you will get push-back because your team will feel that they don't have enough time left in their day to take on the task of delivering more value to each client.

The second reason, of course, comes back to the value and perception of value by your client. If you sit back and wait for your client to approach, you risk losing them to another accountant who is proactive about technology, growth, and bottom line impact. Remember, you are currently charging a rate (whether hourly or fixed) that is based on your inefficiencies. They may perceive your lack of initiative as trying to protect your current pricing structure and this could easily cause them to become more price conscious. Also, you will find it very difficult to build trust/safety and establish your expertise, if your client perceives you as a dinosaur when it comes to technology and business improvement. They will assume it is not safe to deal with you and they will also question the veracity of your proof if they can see that you are still operating in the dark ages.

Let's take a moment to examine how this played out in Andrew's practice...

When he took the time he needed to look closely at his own practice, Andrew realized that every team member had his or her own way of doing things. Some were much more efficient than others. If he wanted to free up capacity so his people could Create Value for his clients, he needed to enlist the support of each of them to systemize, streamline, and automate every single aspect of their working day.

Andrew could easily have gotten distracted by the internal inefficiencies and continued to focus inwardly on costs and his own margins. However, the efficiency metric paled in comparison when contrasted with the need to ensure the effectiveness of delivering the value they had promised their clients. The standardization, automation, and simplification was simply a means to an end (to Create Value and effectively deliver what their clients valued most), and not the end goal in and of itself.

So Andrew brought his team together, to identify all the services they provided and the processes they followed. These included onboarding their clients, completing individual tax returns, doing their monthly accounts, and much more. Then they broke each task down, step by step. Team members shared their distinct approaches, and worked together to identify the most effective ways of completing each task. They sought to minimize errors, and eliminate double-handling, rework, or manual processes. Once they had identified the best approaches, they described the steps involved, and the systems and technology which supported best practices.

Every activity was documented, using either a checklist or template. The team agreed to complete the checklist for each activity before it was reviewed by a manager, sent to a client, or lodged with the tax office. Following these steps reduced the number of errors and re-work to almost zero.

Like a small number of progressive accountancy practices, Andrew had eliminated timesheets when he first transitioned to fixed pricing 12 months earlier. When he introduced Pricing Value, he felt tempted to re-instate the use of timesheets, so that he could measure efficiency during the process of streamlining and automating everything. However, with coaching and accountability he realized that he had to resist this temptation at all costs and focus squarely on building the pricing and value capabilities of his team members instead.

Before long, Andrew had automated and systematized his firm's procedures and key workflows without resorting to time tracking. He could easily see what was or wasn't working and then identify the training and development needs of his people. Andrew continued working with his team to unlock incremental improvements, freeing up even more capacity to devote to Creating Value. Within 60 days, he was ready to move to the next phase and train each team member on the mindset and soft skills required to Comprehend, Create, Capture, and Communicate Value.

Inspired by his success, Andrew then set himself an ambitious new target: to grow revenue by 25 percent. He believed he could do this by creating 25 percent more value for his clients and delivering each engagement in the most effective way possible—as those were the only metrics that actually mattered to his clients.

It is vital to note that the use of timesheets (paper or app based) is a contentious issue in the realm of value-based pricing. Many so-called experts are not clear about why [exactly] time tracking is completely useless in the realm of Pricing Value. Rather than offend anyone, many of these experts will mistakenly tell you that it's ok to hold on to this old bastion of knowledge. Simply put, it isn't.

First and foremost, timesheets have no place in the process of Creating and Capturing Value for a firm that is committed to Pricing Value. Your cost structure and internal productivity are in no way related to the value you are able to create for your clients. If you are at all confused or unsure about this, please go back now and revisit Chapter 6 where we discussed in detail the importance of Capturing a large portion of the Value Created with each client.

If you continue to use timesheets, what you will find is that it will detrimentally impact your ability to make the 180 degree turn required to implement Pricing Value properly. Timesheets are incongruent and incompatible with Pricing Value. This point cannot be stressed enough as this is where 90 percent of your contemporaries are falling down when trying to hold onto time-tracking while transitioning away from cost-based pricing methodologies. Your costs have absolutely no bearing on the discussions you need to have with your clients about value or price. The mindset shifts required to let go of old, outdated thinking, like time tracking, will be examined in greater depth with examples in Chapter 14.

Measure and Monitor Your KPIs

Without a clear strategy and some guidance, you could easily get bogged down in measuring and monitoring your KPIs as you begin to Price Value. Choosing too many (especially the wrong ones) will overwhelm and confuse—which will only make it more challenging for you and your team to focus on what is really important. And make no mistake, it is definitely easy to fall into the trap of measuring the wrong things as there are many pricing consultants who still wrongly advocate the use of timesheets, cost accounting, and so on, to focus inward on practice efficiencies.

Choosing the right KPIs is relatively straightforward once you are clear about where you are in your practice, where you would ideally like to be in 12 months, and what is important to your clients. If you want to Price Value, you must start to measure your firm against the yardstick of what your clients value most. And that is a radical mind shift for most practitioners as most of you have always been focused inward looking at how you can improve the basic numbers, costs, and efficiencies within your firm. It has probably not occurred to you before that what you really should be measuring is the stuff that your clients care about most.

In addition to the question of what to track and measure, there is also the issue of "how many metrics?" As discussed back in Chapter 7, only three or four pieces of information can be processed at once by the part of their brain that decides. Therefore, to maximize focus and clarity, each team member should be given no more than four KPIs to achieve at any given time.

Some of the metrics you should consider as a starting point (not an exhaustive list) to assessing the current health of your practice are:

- Cash flow.
- Practice effectiveness—project delivery, turnaround time, and so on.
- Delivery risk.
- Percentage of income earned via hourly, fixed, and Pricing Value.
- Monthly recurring revenue (MRR) as a percentage of total revenue.
- Value Created for clients and Value Gap.
- Revenue as a percentage of Value Created for your clients.
- Revenue (from engagement amendments due to scope creep) as a percentage of total revenue.
- Compliance revenue as a percentage of total revenue.
- Advisory revenue as a percentage of total revenue.
- Client satisfaction score (NPS) and retention.
- Annual growth in revenue from existing clients.

Now granted, at the beginning of your journey, you may not be able to measure some of these metrics. In fact, it is likely there are a few on this list that you have never contemplated tracking before today. However, this list gives you a good starting point from which to commence your journey, and it also highlights the type of metrics (i.e., leading, customer-behavioral measurements) that you may need to begin capturing and tracking as you transition.

Once you have a clear picture where you are at and where you need more data to illuminate your progress, you can then turn your mind to selecting your initial set of KPIs. Now remember, if you are currently at the beginning of your Pricing Value journey, the metrics you choose initially will be different to those you select six or 12 months in. As you progress further you may begin to swap out those early KPIs with new ones that more accurately track the metrics that really matter to your clients.

Before you proceed to the next section in this chapter, take some time to ponder which three to four KPIs will be most meaningful and impactful to your practice today. Which have you chosen? How will you best measure and track your progress as you commence Pricing Value? What specific targets will each team member be responsible for and how will you empower and influence them to take ownership to achieve them? How will you hold yourself and your team accountable?

What Technology Should You Invest In?

"Whoever heard of an accountant working on New Year's Eve?" Sarah grumbled. Her dining room table should have been covered with a crisp linen tablecloth, so she could set out canapes, champagne glasses and a punch bowl, along with the noisemakers and mistletoe needed to ring in the coming year. Instead, her dining room table was piled high with receipts, invoices, and tax documents. Sarah glanced at her phone: 10:23 a.m. on 31 December. She had precisely six hours and 37 minutes to sort her accounts, enter them into her accounting software, and e-mail them to her accountant before close of business. Otherwise, she faced hefty fines for the late lodgment of her tax return, and her year's end accounts.

How did it come to this? Last New Year's, she had made a resolution. She would update her books every month, rather than leaving everything to the last minute, the way she always did. But old habits die hard. Sarah's accountant had begun with some cheery reminders—no pressure, just letting you know that the sooner we receive your details, the sooner we can lodge your return! Over time, however, the messages had become terser. Her accountant resented her tardiness, because it meant that he needed to work late during the holiday season. Meanwhile, Sarah resented her accountant, for being, well, such an accountant!

Instead of focusing on her pile of receipts, Sarah let her mind wander. She had promised her mother they would spend some quality time together, sharing a quiet drink, reminiscing about the year just past, and dreaming about the year to come. Instead, her mother was sitting across the table, purse-lipped, sorting through Sarah's car expenses. No doubt her mother resented her for being such a procrastinator. Sarah sighed. Her tardiness was going to cost her big time—fines from the tax office, and the silent treatment from her mother.

Perhaps this scenario rings true to you. You've had clients exactly like Sarah. They're busy running their business, so they let their bookkeeping slide for a week or two—and then suddenly it's Christmas, and you don't have the data you need. The same thing happens, year in, year out. A week before filing time they schlep a large bag of receipts into your office and dump it on your desk. Your heart sinks. You know your staff will have to work back to sort the paperwork, and you're dreading the overtime bill.

"I wonder how Felicity is going," Sarah's mother mused. Felicity was one of Sarah's friends from university. She had studied accountancy, and was working as a chartered accountant for a large firm in the city. "She was always so well organized."

Sarah took a deep breath. Typical of her mother to hit below the belt! She was ready to fire back with a sarcastic comment, but bit her tongue. After all, she needed her mother's help. Sarah tapped the screen of her phone again. Four minutes had passed since she last checked the time, and she had accomplished nothing. But Felicity, on the other hand…

Sarah snapped out of her fugue, and smiled at her mother. "You may not realize this," she said, "but that was a brilliant suggestion." She picked up her phone and stepped into the next room to make a call.

"I'm glad one of us is brilliant," Sarah's mother thought.

As soon as she was out of earshot, Sarah dialed Felicity. "Pick up, pick up," she muttered. After four rings, she hears her friend's voice.

"Hi Sarah! How are you enjoying your holidays?"

"Holidays?" Sarah replied. "That's a laugh. I'm up to my neck in receipts, and feel like I'm drowning!"

Felicity chuckled. "Wasn't it the same story last year? And the year before that?"

"Well, yes. But I just feel overwhelmed."

"Let me guess. Your accountant wanted the figures last week?"

"End of November, actually," Sarah admitted.

"OK. This is an emergency. Here's what you need to do. Do you have a pen handy?"

Felicity then introduced Sarah to a great little app. She stepped her through the process of scanning her receipts, or e-mailing electronic receipts to the software. "If you use supplier rules, it will automate the publishing process. You'll have all your data automatically uploaded to your accounting software and ready to send to your accountant before you've mixed champagne cocktails for your Mum and yourself!"

"Are you serious?" Sarah asked. "Why hasn't my accountant shown me how to do this?"

Felicity shrugged. "Some people just don't stay abreast of all the changes in software," she said. From that moment on, Sarah's relationship with her accountant was doomed. Nine years of badgering and last-minute lodgments meant nothing to her anymore.

If you're anything like Sarah's accountant, you may not understand how technology has changed the rules of engagement. Compliance tasks, which once took days to complete, can now be done in hours, or even minutes. Modern software analyses the data you input, identifies your needs, and customizes itself to suit your business. Sure, technology has the power to improve the internal efficiency of your practice, but it offers so much more. It can also streamline the way your clients manage their accounts, and increase the value they perceive in working with you. For example, you can:

- Show your clients how to automatically feed their receipts and bank statements into their accounting software, using apps such as Receipt Bank, AutoEntry, and Hubdoc.
- Speak with clients anywhere in the world, using video-conferencing software such as Skype and Zoom.
- Access your clients' data in real time using cloud-based software, allowing you to proactively manage and guide their business.

Your clients' expectations of you are rapidly changing. The service you provided even three years ago may be woefully inadequate today. Clients want you to keep them up-to-date with new technology. They want you to interpret their data and broader business trends, enabling them to make better decisions. If you're unable to give them what they want, they will find an accountant who better meets their needs. This New Year, Sarah made a different resolution: she would find an accountant who was up to speed with emerging technology, who valued her time as much as she did. This was one resolution she most definitely kept. To her delight, she found that the cloud revolution made it much easier for her to take her business elsewhere.

Before you start choosing the best technology to assist your clients, review Chapter 4—Comprehend Value. Then ask yourself the following questions:

- What are your clients' pain points?
- What keeps them awake at night with worry?
- Where do they need (or want) to get to in their business in the next 12 months?

Once you understand what each client needs and values, you can develop a customized solution for them. Because Sarah had thousands of receipts to sort, a receipt scanning app proved ideal, offering her both speed and ease-of-use. Because Andrew needed to streamline his onboarding process for new clients, a practice management tool like Karbon was an obvious choice. It saved him, on average, six hours set-up time per client. Andrew also calculated the ongoing savings averaged three hours per client, per month. With hundreds of clients, the time savings alone really impacted his practice as it freed up hundreds of hours and capacity each month for Value Creation.

How to Design and Implement a Training Plan

Andrew soon realized that training his staff to Comprehend, Create, Capture, and Communicate Value would be a mammoth task. Initially, he had hoped that individual conversations with each team member would be enough. But the level of confusion he noticed when he spoke with staff initially about Comprehending Value convinced him that he was wrong.

This became a problem that kept Andrew awake at night. One evening, as he glanced across at his bedside clock and realized he had been wide awake for three hours, his mind racing all the while, he experienced an epiphany: what if my staff are also finding it hard to sleep? He reached across to his nightstand, grabbed a notebook, and jotted down the question. Three minutes later, he had fallen into a deep sleep. He dreamed of an office where all his team were on the same page, and woke up feeling refreshed and rejuvenated.

The next morning, he worked on his notes while he munched his breakfast cereal. He realized that the skills, processes, and strategies required to implement Pricing Value would be unfamiliar to his team. These they could learn—but he had to face a much larger problem. Skills and processes were less important than developing the right mindset—one which moved them radically away from the idea of hourly billing, or fixed prices. While he had been busy helping his staff free up the time needed to Create Value, he had failed to make time for himself. And time was essential if he hoped to lead his people through a successful transformation to Pricing Value. Andrew poured himself a coffee, and sat down at his kitchen table to map out his next steps:

1. Identify the end result. What specifically will need to change in the way we approach, communicate with, and onboard clients? How [exactly] will we Create, deliver, and Capture Value?
2. Break down the processes, systems, and elements involved in this new way of working. Then list the different tools or techniques that can support each team member, including:
   • Templates
   • Knowledge
   • Soft skills
   • Training
   • Mindset
3. Allocate time to speak with each team member to assess their current knowledge, skills, and mindset.
   • Relate their current position to the firm's desired outcome.
   • Ask them what they need from me (and other team members) to Price Value for all new and existing clients in 18 months' time.
   • Develop a written education and development plan in conjunction with each team member.
4. Draw together the individual development plans to create a learning plan for the firm.
   • Prioritize the training that is required immediately.
   • Allocate a budget to cover the cost of training.
   • If necessary, engage reputable external providers to conduct parts of the training.

5. Refine the learning plan by asking:
   - What could be covered during a formal training session?
   - What can be learned by observation?
   - What case studies or practical problems could help the team learn the required skills?
   - Can I create templates or checklists to accelerate the learning for my people?
   - Would regular team meetings afford opportunities to share both successes and setbacks, thus accelerating understanding and learning?

Create Templates Required to Comprehend, Create, Capture, and Communicate Value

Given that your learning curve will be steep, it makes sense to create templates or step-by-step guides to help your team members learn how to Price Value systematically.

The best way to create these systems and resources is to ensure you understand each step of the Pricing Value process and then build out your workflows and/or processes. For example, you should consider:

- The best way to attract and qualify your ideal leads (based on your niche).
- The specific questions your team will use to identify and quantify pain points.
- How to establish Economic Value and create unique, valuable solutions that immediately disqualify your competitors.
- How to draft a proposal once the price options have been created and communicated to your client.
- How team members will complete each step of the work required to deliver each solution, and so on.

For each process or workflow, you must break each of the steps down into great detail, including any tools or approvals that are required to do the job. You can easily achieve this by assembling a small but interested work party of team members. Since your team is likely to be the persons carrying out the process, it makes logical sense to involve them in determining the optimal workflows. For each step in question, pause to challenge the ideas, technology, and assumptions put forward—this will ensure you maximize the efficiency of the process that you are designing with your team, and minimize any possibility of error or omission. Once you and your team have agreed upon each process, codify it in a simple, easy to follow template and/or checklist.

If you would like to access tailor-made templates, guidelines, and checklists that have already been tested on accounting practices just like yours, visit pricingvalue.co/workbook to pick up your copy and start implementing Pricing Value today. In addition to exploring real life case studies, you will receive road-tested, step-by-step instructions on how to:

- Prepare your firm for the move to Pricing Value;
- Conduct an impactful exploratory session with a client to Comprehend Value;
- Uncover and establish Economic Value above and beyond the time and materials that go into the solutions you deliver;
- Master effective ways to Capture Value and increase the value of your firm;
- Communicate Value through powerful and persuasive strategies; and
- Draw out, pre-empt, and deal with objections.

CHAPTER 11

How to Decide on Your Firm's Solutions and Prices

"Older generations say that Millennials can't commit to relationships." Natasha's fingers raced across the keyboard of her laptop. "As a Millennial, I'm calling BS on that. I really want a long-term relationship—but it has to deliver what I need."

Natasha pushed back in her chair, and reread the opening lines of her "Dear John" e-mail. Why did some people make it so hard to end a relationship? They often implied that she was the one at fault. She sighed. Dumping an accountant shouldn't be this hard. After all, she's the client, and she's not satisfied. End of story. But with his entitled attitude and passive-aggressive manner, he reminded her of a particularly unpleasant ex-partner.

In the beginning, he had practically promised to fly her to the moon and back. Her accountant, that is—her ex was far less seductive. During their first meeting, her accountant spent 30 minutes telling her how good he was. His knowledge of tax law, his business acumen, the 10 years he spent with one of the Big Four in London and New York. But when Natasha looked back, the entire meeting had been one extended advertisement for his firm. Not once did he ask about her business. He didn't bother to ask what she needed, or wanted to achieve. No wonder she decided to sever the relationship. "Perhaps I'll need to organize a restraining order for my cloud accounting data," she mused.

Natasha understood restraining orders. After qualifying in Law, she worked with a boutique firm specializing in family law. Several years later she moved west for family reasons. Taking a deep breath, she decided to hang out her shingle, and start her own practice. Although it took a while to build momentum, she now enjoyed a steady stream of clients, enough to support her, a junior lawyer, two administrative staff, and an external accountant who refused to pull his own weight.

Although Natasha should have been prospering, she was struggling to pay her bills each month. Many of her clients were short on cash, and could not pay until their cases were settled. Unlike the boutique firm for which she had previously worked, Natasha extended credit to her hard-luck cases. Her cash-flow suffered as a result. She had also paid a web developer to build an e-commerce site for her, so she could sell some of her DIY legal templates online. While the site looked beautiful, Natasha had not been able to gain the level of traffic or sales that she needed to justify the cost of development.

In addition, Natasha wanted to build her practice up further, but felt nervous about borrowing the money she needed to do so. She wanted an accountant who would partner with her, help her develop the best family law practice on the West Coast, and inform her of possible problems before they arose. Paying good money for someone to basically just perform the grunt work of lodging tax returns and financial reports felt like a lost opportunity to her.

Before Natasha hit Send on her e-mail, she decided to conduct a little more research. After all, no one should change their accountant more frequently than their designer handbag. The first thing she noticed, after scanning a few websites, was that 99 percent of accountants were happy to take on any clients, provided they had a pulse—and the ability to pay. They were trying to be all things to all people. They would work with sole traders, partnerships, small businesses, and startups, and were quick to list all the services they could provide. But none of them offered the help and advice she really wanted, such as:

- Having a deep appreciation for the challenges faced by legal practices such as hers (including those which sold online services).
- Being connected with specialists who could assist her with other critical issues, such as SEO and online conversion rates.
- Offering monthly phone calls to check in, answer any questions she might have, and offer proactive advice to help her grow safely.
- Understanding the specific cash flow problems she was facing, and providing strategies to overcome them.

- Using cloud-based technology to simplify her bookkeeping, payroll and other chores, giving her more free time to focus on improving her business.
- Reviewing her accounting package each month to make sure her e-commerce apps and bank feeds were up-to-date and fit for purpose.
- Offering a quick turnaround of services for those times when she had to meet a looming deadline.

After clicking through dozens of websites, Natasha's eyeballs felt like they had been rubbed with fine-grit sandpaper. She sensed the anger rising in her chest. Every accountant offered to take her business to the next level using value-added packages. She thought to herself "what are they talking about?" These were supposedly small-business specialists who seemingly had no insight or clue about the real challenges faced by legal practices like hers. It was as if every single accountant had hired the same 18-year-old, green web developer to create and put up their website. Every site used the same uninspiring pitch, impenetrable accounting jargon, and timeworn sales clichés.

The net result? She decided that none of them could meet her needs.

Natasha was prepared to pay well for the right accountant—someone who understood her needs as the owner of an emerging legal practice. Someone who would work shoulder-to-shoulder with her to achieve the massive expansion she had planned for the next five years. She longed for someone she could turn to as a trusted advisor and who would be there with her for the long haul.

And it's not just Natasha who has this problem with generic accounting websites, social media posts, and marketing materials. If you just take 20 minutes out of your busy day to critically compare your website with your competitors, you will discover that your site isn't distinguishable from your competition. But even more importantly, if you can't tell the difference, how is your ideal client supposed to differentiate and choose you?

Before you can Price Value, you must decide on a tightly defined target market—sometimes referred to by marketing professionals as a niche. It is impossible to become a master at Comprehending and Creating Value for ALL business owners. In order to set yourself apart and break the deadly cycle of competing based on price, you need to become a world class expert at curing the pain points of a very specific target market. The more proficient you are at identifying, quantifying, and curing pain points for your niche, the higher the premium you will be able to command.

That is why the next step in the process of Pricing Value is to decide on WHO (exactly) your ideal customer is.

How to Define Your Target Market

The complex art of defining your ideal customer (aka your target market or niche) involves:

- identifying clients that you are passionate about working with,
- having confidence that it is narrow (yet deep) enough for you to make a good living from it, and
- ascertaining that you have the expertise to create unique solutions that cure pain points for this ideal client, and automatically disqualify your competitors.

The best way to define and narrow down your target market is to follow this simple 5 Step Process:

1. Create a Wish List
   Ask yourself "who do you want to do business with?" Be as specific as you can. Identify the geographic range, types of customers, size of businesses (if applicable), and the key elements/characteristics that identify them.
2. Identify Pain
   Clarify the specific pain that your ideal customer is in. Educated guesses or assumptions based solely on experience will often not produce the required amount of clarity. You may need to do a lot more research in order to determine exactly what keeps him/her up at night.
3. Assess Expertise
   Remember, it's not enough to accurately diagnose the pain of your audience, you must show that you can cure that pain—and prove it.

If your prospect doesn't believe that it will work, he or she simply won't buy from you. At this stage, it is imperative to critically assess whether you have the required expertise and proof to deliver solutions to cure these specific pain points.

4. Fusion

By this stage, your niche should have begun to take shape as your solution and your client's pain converge to produce a highly targeted, unique, and magical opportunity. A good niche has five key qualities:

- It takes you where you want to go—in other words, it allows you to grow sustainably and cost effectively.
- Customers want it—meaning, you've hit the pain nail directly on the head.
- It's carefully planned.
- It's unique and cannot easily be replicated by someone else— it immediately disqualifies your competitors.
- It evolves, allowing you to expand in the future.

5. Test and Measure

Once you have a match between niche and your proposed solution, you must test market by giving your ideal customers the opportunity to buy and give you feedback. Testing is important—it doesn't make sense after all the work you have done to cut corners and skip this phase.

As a result of doing your homework, you will be left with a list of potential opportunities to specialize in servicing. Before you proceed further to pare your list down, here are some salient and poignant guidelines:

- It is better to execute a specialty in one niche well, rather than spread your finite resources too thin and tackle more than you can handle.
- Each target market will require its own suite of unique solutions, tech stack, marketing plan, landing page, communications materials, team training plan, and budget.
- Target markets, and the solutions you provide to those markets, must be defined narrowly enough to immediately disqualify your competitors.

- Every team member who engages with clients will require education and mentoring for each target market chosen.

By now, your niche should be coming into focus, along with the pressing problems your clients are facing. An effective niche melds your expertise with your clients' needs. It has the following symbiotic qualities:

- Insight—you have accurately identified and quantified your clients' pain points
- Clarity—you have defined the boundaries of your niche and your plan for expansion
- Uniqueness—the services you offer cannot easily be replicated, thereby immediately disqualifying your competitors
- Prosperity—your niche is sufficiently large and well-funded, allowing you to grow your business in a sustainable manner
- Opportunity—as your niche evolves your business has room to expand.

Having clarified your potential niche, it's time to zoom in and identify the optimum target market for your practice. To do so, ask these simple but powerful questions:

Test 1: Are you passionate about this target market and do you enjoy working with them? Is it specific enough? How could you make it more specific?

Test 2: Can you provide unique and powerful solutions that cure the top three pain points that keep your ideal clients up at night?

Test 3: Is there a good geographical fit between your firm and this target market? Can you serve them with a high degree of value and personalization from where you are?

After putting each of your potential targets through this three-step test, you should be left with one specific market where you have a high degree of expertise and fit. Ideally, you should aim for the triangulation point—the point where the three circles overlap (in Figure 11.1). This

Lawyers that work with clients face
to face and offer online SaaS products
–tech, automation, funding,
and cash flow pain points

Emerging legal practice +
eCommerce apps selling
DIY legal templates
in Northern California

Your skill set

Good

Client specifics

BEST   Triangulation=BEST   Niche that is
unassailable

Good   Good

Geographical
location

San Francisco

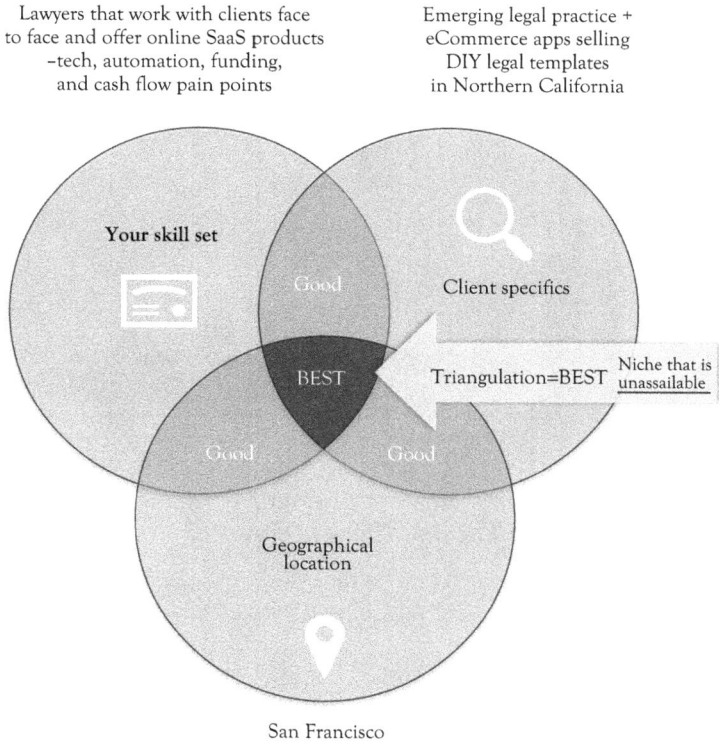

Figure 11.1 Finding a Niche That Is Unassailable

is where you have the BEST chance of creating solutions for your ideal
client that immediately disqualify your competition.

If at this point you still have more than one potential target market where you have achieved maximum overlap, it's time to reduce your
choices further. The best way to approach this task is to plot them on a
graph with *Ease to Win and Service* on the Y axis and *Financial Reward for
Your Firm* on the X axis. The best candidate for your initial target market
(niche) will offer the maximum reward and the greatest ease to win and
service combination (i.e., point C on Figure 11.2).

While it is tempting to take on more than one niche, you should be
mindful that a significant investment will be required to execute each one
masterfully. As a result, one target market is the optimal choice for most
firms starting out on the journey to Price Value.

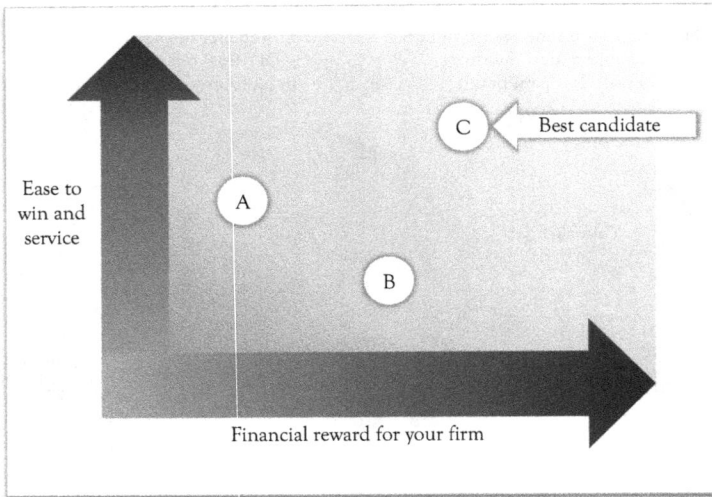

Figure 11.2 Selecting The Best Niche to Focus On

Research

You might believe you already know your target market inside out. Even so, more research will always pay large dividends. There is always more to discover and there are many different ways to find out more about your chosen target markets:

- Read widely:
  - Trade press
  - Newsletters
  - Websites
  - Blogs and podcasts (follow the thought leaders in your chosen field)
  - Reports
  - Social media (LinkedIn, Twitter, Facebook, Instagram, and so on)
  - White papers
- Participate in online forums and discussion groups.
- Attend relevant industry events, such as conferences and seminars.

- Run focus groups for people within the industry or clients of your target market.
- Send out a survey or questionnaire.
- Interview prospects and clients within your identified target market.

Once you have gained a working knowledge of your target market, you may feel tempted to stop researching. This would be a mistake because the key factors affecting your target market can change rapidly: the economy, technology, legislation, competition, and so on. Set a little time aside each week to keep abreast of any changes as they occur.

Conducting Client Interviews

You have three clear goals to keep in mind when you are conducting your research. First, what are the pain points that keep your ideal clients up at night? Or where do they need to get to in order to achieve their ideal vision for the future? Second, what are the key characteristics that all of your ideal prospects have common? And third, how motivated are they to acquire the solution now?

The answers to these questions will help you create client personas (also known as avatars)—to be discussed in depth later on in this chapter. These avatars will help to make your firm's marketing communications and content captivating and persuasive to your niche.

First, here's how to engage with your clients, so they will agree to meet with you and also gain value from the time that you spend with them:

- Remember, it's not actually about YOU. Invite them to share what their biggest challenges are and their dreams/plans for the future. Keep it focused on them and not on your need to understand them purely because you want to sell something to them.
- Don't ask for too much too soon. Most people will say "yes" to a 15-minute chat and then gladly extend that time further if they are receiving great value or clarity from the discussion.

Here are some questions that you can use to get the conversation flowing and uncover priceless information about your ideal clients:

- What is the number one challenge that you are facing right now?
- How is it impacting what you do at an individual, functional, and organizational level?
- What is the top barrier to growth?
- What is the biggest threat to your future success?

Research is vital to your ability to Price Value. The more you practice your skills at Comprehending Value by interviewing your existing and potential clients, the more adept and knowledgeable you will become. To start, you must conduct at least 10–15 interviews with clients or prospects that fit your ideal target market. Keep detailed notes of what you hear and plot the answers in a spreadsheet—this will help to visually illuminate trends in the information that you are gleaning about pain points and value. Ideally, every team member that is client facing should receive education and mentorship to hone this invaluable skill. The ability to Comprehend Value is a must-have skill for a modern accountant, not merely an option.

What Is an Avatar and How Will It Help You?

A client persona (or avatar) is a fictionalized version of your ideal client. It will help you develop marketing strategies or client communications that captivate and persuade your target market. Visualizing your ideal client's characteristics and pain points via an avatar essentially humanizes your marketing.

An avatar will also inspire and guide you and your team as they interact with clients. It forces you to visualize the characteristics and pain points of your ideal client in your mind so that when you craft a message or speak to a potential client that fits that avatar, you are much more likely to say things that will capture their attention and draw them in toward you. In a nutshell, it personalizes and gives more depth to your team's understanding of each target market group. It also helps you to create materials that resonate at a deep, old-brain level with your target market.

Here's how to create a vivid, compelling avatar for each of your ideal clients:

- Identify some of the core characteristics shared by the majority of clients in your target market. These may include (but not be limited to):
  o Gender and family circumstances
  o Physical appearance
  o Age and education levels
  o Approach to their business
  o Lifestyle, hobbies, and pop culture references
  o Personalities
- Create a character that blends these aspects into one compelling, highly visual personality that you and your team can relate to
- Give the avatar a real name that means something to you and your team (Note: this name is for internal use only)
- Develop anecdotes that show how your avatar interacts with his or her:
  o Customers, colleagues, and suppliers
  o Accountant and tax authorities
  o Family

The more color and detail you can build around your client personas, the better. If you have identified trades people as your niche for example, you may consider an avatar called "Tim the Tool Man Taylor." You see, a tradesman can look like different things to different people. But for those of you who are old enough to have seen the TV show Home Improvement, Tim the Tool Man is a funny, down-to-earth craftsman, with a wife and three kids, who lives in a middle-class suburb, and drives a Ford pickup truck. When you mention Tim the Tool Man, everyone on your team can picture him clearly in their mind. This also makes it much easier to think of client stories, pictures, explanations, and anecdotes that would appeal to someone like Tim.

Here's one simple example of how you might put an avatar like this to work at your firm...

Tim the Tool Man doesn't enjoy bookkeeping and on the surface he may come across as a guy who is not on top of the key numbers in his business. Some accountants may even be tempted to avoid getting into a discussion with him about cash flow, even though it's a crucial topic. But if you think about it, Tim can estimate a kitchen refit or complete makeover by whipping out his laser tape measure, a pencil, and a notebook. He can sum up the cost of labor and materials in his head, and he will develop a comprehensive list of all the materials required on the spot. His estimates are 95 percent accurate. So Tim is no dummy when it comes to numbers and measurement—he just uses his mind differently than you do.

Once you and your team understand this subtle nuance, you can use this avatar and knowledge to build a much stronger relationship with clients who reflect his characteristics. You can even use what you now know about "how his mind works" to create visuals, props, stories, and anecdotes that will allow you to position, communicate, and deliver your cash flow solutions in an old-brain friendly way to Tim or any client like him. Having this degree of precision and persuasiveness in your client communications will make it even tougher for competitors to duplicate what you do.

Once you have developed the avatars for your niche and nailed the top three pain points for each, you can then turn your mind to creating the unique and differentiated solutions that will become the core foundation of your practice.

How to Create Solutions Your Clients Value

If you are like most small accounting firms, you probably earn the bulk of your revenue from compliance—tax returns, bookkeeping, and year end accounts. Statistically speaking, increasing the value you capture for compliance services will give the biggest boost to your cash flow (i.e., the 80/20 rule or Pareto Principle applies).

Unfortunately, even though compliance services make up the bulk of your practice, your clients don't value these tasks highly. By law, they must account for their income and expenditure. However, completing tax returns does not help your clients grow or improve their businesses.

Because your clients lodge their tax returns with gritted teeth, compliance work is notoriously difficult to price based on value. They will often quibble about the price, or demand to know why your competitor down the street can do it cheaper.

It is fairly easy to quote a fixed price on compliance work to ensure you earn more than you did with an hourly rate, but it is much more difficult to Price Value. To Price Value on a compliance task, you need to work much harder to niche down and then establish the Economic Value that was covered in Chapter 5. The only way that you can Create Value and price it in the context of compliance is if you can cure pain points (some of you may think of this as advisory) and uncover Economic Value above and beyond the time and materials that go into creating the solution.

Remember, your compliance work is a lot like the glass of water that we spoke about in Chapter 1. The value of having a drink (or getting the tax return completed) is different for every client, depending on how thirsty they are at the moment. In order to create a stable of in-demand, unique solutions that cure the key pain points for your ideal client and render you the only sane choice, you need to have intimate knowledge of the depth of their thirst, as well as the deal-breakers. Like the example in Chapter 5, you must uncover the key factors (i.e., the order-taking software going down regularly and resulting in lost sales) that render the price a non-issue.

So let's consider an obvious example such as a tax return. Your job is to ask the questions that your competitors won't (or are afraid to) ask, in order to uncover the deal-breakers for your ideal client. For example you might ask:

- When you think of hiring an accountant to complete your tax return, what is the #1 impediment that you encounter?
- Why is that important to you?
- If that happened (or didn't happen) what would be the consequences to you?

Once you know what the key deal-breakers are in your client's mind, you can use that information to Create Value in your solution to command a premium price. These things could include quick turnaround, involvement of specific personnel in the preparation of the return, technology to simplify data collation by your client, audit insurance, and so on.

The key point is simple: the actual preparation of the tax return under both scenarios (fixed or value-based pricing) will likely involve roughly the same amount of hours and materials. However, in the scenario where you have uncovered significant deal-breakers and leveraged them to Price Value, you have put yourself in a position to Create and Capture more Value.

Yes, it is possible to Price Value in the context of compliance tasks but it cannot be achieved by an app or a spreadsheet. It is incumbent upon you to create enough Economic Value to render price a non-issue.

As you discovered in Chapter 5, bundling is also a very effective technique for Pricing Value with what might normally be considered compliance-type tasks. As George Loewenstein discovered in 2005, buyers prefer the simplicity of one purchase rather than having to transact multiple times to acquire separate services.[1] Multiple transactions require multiple decisions, and as you learned way back in Chapter 2, decision making fatigues the brain. In essence, more decisions means more pain for your client. Bundling reduces buying friction because it is old-brain friendly.

Therefore, when you think about the solutions that you will design and present to your ideal clients, it makes sense to bundle up the inescapable compliance tasks with bespoke solutions that address their most pressing pain points. You need to stop thinking of compliance and advisory as separate aspects of your practice. You are no longer in the business of pumping out compliance services, with the odd interesting advisory project. If you start thinking about and viewing your practice as a holistic, one-stop business improvement shop, you will find it much easier to create solutions that your clients value highly. Plus, you will have the added benefit of deriving confidence and personal satisfaction from delivering more value, and being appreciated for what you do.

---

[1] Camerer, C., G. Loewenstein, and D. Prelec. March 2005. "Neuroeconomics: How Neuroscience Can Inform Economics." *Journal of Economic Literature* 43, no. 1, pp. 9–64.

By the end of this process, you should aim to have a small portfolio of unique solutions for each of the key pain points that each avatar in your niche has. Later, you will use these solutions as the core foundation for constructing the package offerings that you present to each client. Remember, if you have selected more than one niche (target market) for your firm, you will need to repeat this entire process again for each of your niches.

How to Price Your Packages

It's tempting to review your competitors' websites, to source cues to formulate your firm's pricing. Unfortunately, this strategy will only lead to confusion and price competition—it will actually take your attention away from focusing on finding the optimal price that each ideal client is willing to pay for your unique solutions to his or her most pressing pain points.

A firm that is correctly Pricing Value will never quote an exact price for solutions on their website. Each client must be priced individually. You cannot possibly anticipate what is of value to a potential client until you sit down and go through the process of Comprehending Value.

Your aim with each client is to offer a small selection (three is the ideal number for all the reasons discussed in Chapters 7 and 9) in a face-to-face meeting. You will price these three options from high to low. Your highest priced option (referred to as your "A" offering, as discussed in Chapter 9) will provide the most complete (premium) solution to the pain points that your client has identified.

As a guide, you may want to avail yourself of a quoting or proposal tool to help give you a ballpark idea of what some of the compliance components might be worth. However, these tools cannot give you a value-based price—they can only give you an estimate of a fixed price for the compliance components. The biggest risk with using one of these apps is that they are a constant reminder of the tools and mindset that you were lugging around on your back when you were trying to outrun the fire of price competition. You cannot outrun that fire with the logic, approach and mindset that created the problem in the first place.

And it is also crucial to note that the compliance aspects of your engagements are only a tiny component of the overall value that you now must deliver. Once you commit to Pricing Value in your practice, your primary aim will always be to provide a holistic solution that delivers significant value for your client. And that value of course must be quantified by you personally via the process of Comprehending, Creating, and Communicating Value.

While you've been busy identifying your target market and creating your firm's solutions, Natasha decided to cast her net a bit wider. Instead of a Google search, she took a radical step and asked for recommendations on Linkedin for accountants with experience scaling a modern legal practice. To her surprise, she quickly discovered Melissa in a nearby city. Natasha completed the online form and booked a meeting with Melissa using Zoom.

You will be pleased to hear that Melissa focused on Natasha, rather than herself. She asked probing and thought provoking questions, listened to Natasha's answers, and expertly uncovered Natasha's pain points. Melissa then proposed a strategy to increase Natasha's productivity and effectiveness by implementing leading-edge apps to automate and streamline all of the routine and mundane tasks. Melissa skillfully bundled up all of the compliance work that needed to done but focused the bulk of their conversation on the Economic Value that she could create by offering tangible, bespoke solutions to the stuff that really kept Natasha up at night worrying. She took the time to fundamentally understand what Natasha valued and also where she saw her practice growing and evolving to in the next 3 to 5 years.

After she concluded the meeting, Natasha gave an exuberant fist pump. Sure, she had agreed to pay Melissa three times the amount she had paid her previous accountant, but she had gained more than just an accountant. She had acquired a partner who would help grow her legal practice over the next five years and hold her accountable to her ambitious goals. In her eyes, the sky was the limit.

Natasha clicked on the Drafts folder in her e-mail program, opened her "Dear John" letter to her accountant, and clicked Send. For the first time in eighteen months, she knew she would sleep soundly that night.

Testing Your Price Points

By and large, the price your clients say they will pay is always vastly different from the price they will pay in reality. That is why the first rule of Pricing Value (in Chapter 9) is that you don't talk about your prices.

The only way to know if the prices you have put forward are right or not is to test them with real clients. If the client balks at the price options, then you must ask them to select the specific solutions they are willing to remove or de-prioritize. You will then remove those solutions from the packages (as applicable), reset your prices, and test them again with that client.

When you are testing prices, focus on your client's priorities to cure pain points, rather than the price of any individual element. Allow your clients to select the solutions that meet their needs. Remember what you learned back in Chapter 9 from the pricing adventures of Turing Pharmaceuticals and *The Times*. It may very well be more lucrative for you to convert 5 percent of your enquiries who are prepared to pay $20,000 a year, than 90 percent of your enquiries who are only prepared to pay $2,000 a year.

When it comes to Pricing Value, over thinking is the quickest path to failure.

Pricing Ad Hoc Services and Advisory Services

Picture the scene…your client rings up in a blind panic. She needs a set of management accounts done for the bank so her mortgage application can be granted. If she can't present these accounts by close of business tomorrow, she'll lose out on the dream house she's got her heart set on.

This scenario presents a unique opportunity to Price Value for some urgent bespoke work. Your client imagines her dream house slipping through her fingers, so her pain is intense. You will have to set other important work aside to meet her deadline. But how often do you as the accountant miss your chance to Capture Value in a scenario like this, by simply quoting a fixed price off the top of your head?

Pricing Value for ad hoc or advisory services is actually much more straightforward than pricing compliance work, because you are not as constrained mentally by the cost structure of your practice. You can clearly see the opportunity to provide real value for your client.

But the challenge still remains: what should you actually charge? And how do you make sure that your team is trained up to consistently Price Value in these scenarios?

The key to Pricing Value for advisory work is to use the system—starting with the 6 Cs. First and foremost, you must control your own fear and mindset around your "worth." When your client is panicking, it's easy to fall into the trap of premature quotation. But remember, in Chapter 3 you learned that your thoughts and fears have a direct impact on your results. While it's tempting to use the tools and strategies that you have always used in the past, they are next to useless to you now that the game has changed completely.

The Pricing Value system is your "escape fire" plan. Take your time to fully Comprehend Value by developing a clear appreciation of the issues that are important to your client, and why. Determine what the cost of doing nothing (or in the example above, the cost of not meeting the deadline) is for your client. Next, establish the clear Economic Value of your unique solution and Communicate Value clearly to your client using the strategies discussed in Chapter 7. Lay the foundation to Convince with each step as you work your way through the system. Always remember that the key to building a valuable practice is learning how to Capture a portion of the Value that you Create for your client.

And just a few final thoughts on this topic—you may also want to consider:

1. Having a base "do not go below price" is essential for each unique solution and every client. These thresholds should be reviewed regularly and increased at a minimum, annually.
2. Using a multiplier (1.5x or 2x) for any services that require a very quick turnaround time or where a specific practitioner is requested to work on the engagement.
3. Scaling up pricing in bands based on the size of business you are dealing with.
4. If you propose a retrospective or success rate (i.e., for jobs where you help a client access finance or close a sale), what will the percentage

be? Will you utilize a TIP clause—essentially allow the client to pay you based upon their satisfaction with the results that you achieve? Will the entire remuneration be at risk or only a portion (i.e., a base rate plus a TIP clause)?

CHAPTER 12

How to Re-value All Your Existing Clients

"I know why so many of my clients drink too much," Brad thought to himself. "Because managing cash flow is a nightmare." He reviewed his accounts receivable and payable for the coming month, then double-checked his bank balance. No, a miracle had not occurred during the last 20 seconds. He was still $25,000 in the hole. Brad's stomach lurched. Swamped with work, his people were demanding more resources, but how could he afford another employee? Mutinous grumblings were spreading through his team. Where did it all go so wrong?

Three years ago, Brad had a vision of a new type of accounting practice. He envisaged a cloud-only firm, not constricted by legacy systems or outdated thinking. Grasping the opportunities offered by emerging technologies, he built a highly efficient cloud-based practice centered around his clients' needs. He relished the chance to build a new type of firm—one that his former partners, with their antiquated ways, just could not imagine.

Eager to grow his practice quickly, Brad hit the market with bold claims and aggressive pricing. His name drew clients through the door, and his all-inclusive packages sealed the deal. His business expanded so rapidly that it took him two years to see the critical mistake he had made. Setting his prices too low just wasn't sustainable. His oldest clients, who had supported him from the start, were choking off his cash flow. Maybe—just maybe—he could have survived another year but his operating costs had blown out exponentially. When his lease terminated, he had no choice but to move to more expensive premises; a senior staff member quit, and his firm's public indemnity insurance skyrocketed. It was, Brad concluded, the perfect storm.

He knew he had to hike the prices for his legacy clients. But how could he wean them off their low priced, all-you-can-eat packages? He expected plenty of kick-back. And on a personal level, he felt conflicted. These clients had backed him years ago when all he had was a dream, a laptop, and a name they could trust. Most of them were like family to him.

Some elements of Brad's story may resonate with you, while others may not. However, there's every chance that you're carting along some legacy clients, that you can no longer afford to carry. You may also need to upsize your revenue from these clients—but you probably dread sitting down with them and initiating what you believe will be an extremely difficult conversation.

Conquer Your Fear

Like many of you, Brad was deliberately avoiding the "price conversation" with his initial clients because of his deep seated fear (or belief) that he could lose a large number of them. The thought of losing clients, especially the 35 that came on board early and were extremely loyal, troubled him a lot. He therefore convinced himself that it was much more effective to just focus on Pricing Value with new clients. The only downside was, he was actually losing a lot of money servicing those early clients, and each year they became a bigger drain on his cash flow. It eventually got to the point where he could no longer ignore the evidence that the legacy clients were killing his practice, and re-valuing their engagements became a non-negotiable. As you might expect, even though he knew it had to be done to keep his practice afloat, he was gripped with trepidation, and he could not bring himself to actually do it.

And therein lies the dilemma…

Knowing *rationally* that you need to have a crucial conversation with your clients is one thing, but being able to face your fears and get it done is quite another. If you have come to the realization, based on what you have read so far, that the pricing for your existing clients is both under value and unsustainable, then you are likely to have a number of thoughts, beliefs, habits, excuses, and fears flooding through your mind. This is completely normal. Let's examine some of the more common mental hurdles together and assess what you can do, despite these obstacles, to move forward confidently.

When you think about moving all of your clients to Pricing Value, what are the thoughts, beliefs, habits, excuses, or fears that come up for you? In your mind, what is the main issue that prevents you from converting 100 percent of your existing clients, right now?

To help you with this important exercise, here's a list of some common reasons that accountants give for delaying (or refusing to) implement Pricing Value with existing clients:

- What if I lose all my clients or even just a large percentage of them?
- What if my clients become angry and lash out at me about the increase?
- How can I Price Value if I don't have time to learn HOW to do it properly?
- Aren't I better off just finding new clients to Pricing Value with?
- I'm not good with confrontation and I can see myself botching it up completely.
- Will my client think less of me if I admit I have been under-charging for years?
- Am I really worth it? What if I can't deliver?
- All of my clients are price conscious so they are never going to agree to pay more.
- My clients are like friends/family and I feel bad about increasing their price.
- Some of my clients may need to pay significantly more—they will never agree to this.
- I've tried to put my prices up before and it didn't work. How is this going to be any different?

Which of these common fears (or beliefs) resonate with you most?

Before you can begin to implement Pricing Value properly, you must deal with and overcome your own stinking thinking. It's common and normal to have fears and concerns, and to some extent they are justified because Pricing Value is not as simple as "just putting your prices up." If it were, every accountant would already be doing it.

However, just like Hobson and Clarke from Chapter 3, it's what you do now, despite your fear, that is going to define your trajectory of success.

As you discovered earlier, you cannot use rational thought to think your way out of fear. The only cure is exposure. You must face your fear(s) and take action.

Perhaps not surprisingly, Brad was in exactly the same position that you now find yourself in. Here is what he did to move forward confidently.

He first sought out a coach—someone who listened to his fears and excuses, and then helped him to question the thinking, perspective, and assumptions they were based on. You probably won't be surprised to hear that through this process, Brad discovered that 99 percent of the stuff that was holding him back wasn't based in fact or supported by evidence. It was mostly just perceived limitations and negative beliefs that he created in his mind, without any real corroboration. Once he began to pick apart the rules and assumptions behind his head trash, the grip that it had on him magically melted away, and he was able to move forward freely to Price Value.

He also spent some time getting crystal clear about the outcome that he wanted to achieve with the existing clients (especially the 35 he knew he was losing money servicing). This exercise allowed him to realize that even though the price was about to increase, so too was the value that he would be responsible for delivering on the engagements. Seeing this from a win-win perspective, made it easier for him to begin Pricing Value with existing clients.

Do the Math

If you remember, one of Brad's biggest fears at the beginning of his journey was that he couldn't afford to lose existing clients. That fear was exacerbated by the fact his cash flow was in the toilet at the time.

Ironically, you've probably got the exact same fear. It would hurt if a large number of your existing clients left. Could you survive if 30 percent of your clients walked out the door?

The truth is, right now, you don't actually know for sure. You don't know how many clients might leave and you don't know how many clients you could afford to lose.

And if you are being honest, it's hard to make good decisions when you don't have all the information, isn't it?

If you take some time to analyze what you make off each of your clients, you may just find that the data tells a very different story to the one that your fear has fabricated.

If you've been in practice for awhile, the reality is that your existing clients are likely to tick some or all of these boxes:

- Take a disproportionate amount of time to service.
- Contribute less to cash flow than newer clients.
- Often delay in delivering information and put your team under strain to meet deadlines.
- Are difficult to deal with and slow to pay their invoices.
- Constantly complain about the price or ask for freebies and discounts.

When Brad sat down and analyzed his practice, he was horrified to discover that 35 of his legacy clients contributed less than 15 percent of his turnover, and only 5 percent of his cash flow. As you can imagine, Brad was in shock and he contemplated sitting down and having a stiff drink. Furthermore, after taking into consideration the extra software costs and inevitable write offs, he suspected that he could almost afford to fire all 35, and still come out ahead.

The truth is, despite what your fear suggests, the reality is that you don't yet have enough data to know how many clients you might lose (or how many you can afford to lose) if you were to Price Value for all existing client engagements. The only way to know for sure is for you to review your entire portfolio of clients.

How to Complete a Client Review

When it comes to your existing clients, some may face a large increase and others may only need a bit of an adjustment to their pricing to bring it in line with the value created via the engagement. Your strategy for handling each of these scenarios will be different.

If, after going through the process of Comprehending and Creating Value, the overall increase is only going to be a nominal amount, it will largely go unnoticed if you can clearly communicate the incremental value directly to your client. You will do this by focusing squarely on the Economic Value of your proposed solution, and making sure that you involve your client in every step of the Pricing Value process.

Where the price increase is going to be material (i.e., 25+ percent), you will need to work smarter at laying out the proverbial breadcrumbs via the Pricing Value system to ensure you have correctly identified and quantified pain, provided a solution that can cure it, and provided sufficient proof. It is imperative that your client feels they are in control of the priorities to cure each pain point and they must clearly see and acknowledge the cost of continuing to ignore these problems in their business. To successfully raise the price by a significant amount, your client must clearly see the value is commensurate with the increase. In a nutshell, you must increase the value component first, before you can offer packages that bear a higher price.

But before you can work out which client needs which strategy, you need to review your entire portfolio of clients. This exercise will allow you to examine and clarify where the best opportunities lie in your practice to Price Value with existing clients.

Let's walk through the review that Brad conducted on his practice to give you an understanding of what you need to do in yours.

He began by creating a spreadsheet. In Column A, he listed his 35 legacy clients—those who were still on unsustainable fixed packages.

In Column B, he identified each client's business sector using broad categories, such as hospitality, IT, personal services, professional services, charity, retail, and trades.

In Column C, he noted the structure of each client's business: were they sole traders, a partnership, a limited liability company, a not for profit, or some other legal entity?

In Column D, he noted the size of the business—with micro businesses employing fewer than 10 people, small employing 10 to 49, medium-size with 50 to 249 employees, and large with more than 250.

In Column E, he noted the lifecycle stage of the business: startup, no growth, growth, high growth, mature, or in decline.

In Column F, he identified the current services he provided. Did he manage their bookkeeping, sales tax, yearend accounts, tax returns, payroll, managerial accounting, or company compliance, and so on?

In Column G, he identified the Relationship Manager—the staff member responsible for interacting with the client.

In Column H, Brad considered each client's potential to refer new clients to his firm. He categorized them as having low, medium, or high potential for referrals.

In Column I, he assessed the value of each client to his firm. While a client may prove valuable (or costly!) in many different ways, Brad defined his grading system like this:

(a) Clients who are strategically important. They may be paying high prices or directly relevant to his plan for growth over the next three to five years.
(b) Clients who had the potential to move into category A.
(c) Small but cash flow positive clients that were unlikely to grow.
(d) Cash flow negative clients, those who were difficult to work with, or tardy with their payments.

Once Brad had completed his list, he noticed that three quarters of his legacy clients were in the building trades. Some were up to 90 days behind in their payments to him, others were argumentative, and some were just unwilling to take advice. "Time to sack a few of them," Brad thought. Then he looked a little closer at his spreadsheet and he began to see some insights that completely transformed the way he looked at and operated his practice.

Virtually all his tradesman clients were sole traders or small operators. In most cases, their wives were trying to manage all the bookkeeping and payroll out of a home office, while simultaneously taking care of young children. They all engaged Brad to clean up the files, correct any mistakes, and file their returns. He knew that his clients hated all the paperwork, and the time it took. Brad opened up a couple of client files, and checked their cash flow. They weren't just late paying him—they were late paying their suppliers, their workers, and the tax office. Why? Because their customers were consistently late paying them. When he delved deeper, Brad realized that many of his clients were also not getting get the invoices out to the customers in a timely fashion either which led to more delays. These rookie mistakes left most of his tradesmen teetering on the edge of bankruptcy. These guys may have been great at plumbing but the plumbing in their business was grossly substandard—they were leaking cash flow profusely.

The metaphoric lightbulb went off in Brad's mind. Without realizing it, he had stumbled across some of the potential key pain points for these clients—and some powerful, valuable solutions. And he realized that he'd probably let them down and judged them as not being great clients, when it was he who could easily have stepped in and helped them with solutions that were much more valuable than just cleaning up their bookkeeping mess and filing returns.

Brad realized that it wasn't enough to make a list like he did in Columns A to I and to judge the value or potential value of each client based on factors that are only relevant to the old way that he used to operate his firm. If Brad wanted to Price Value, he needed to stop looking at the relationship as purely transactional and measurable by purely accounting terms such as contribution or profit margins. He needed to start looking at it through the eyes of a relational lens—he needed to start measuring what the client valued and evaluate each client's potential based on his firm's ability to deliver highly relevant and valuable solutions to those specific pain points.

As a result, he added two more columns to his spreadsheet (Columns J and K) to accommodate the key pain points and also the bespoke solutions they could deliver, that immediately disqualified competitors (see Table 12.1).

Completing this exercise helped to strengthen his resolve to price these clients based on the value brought to the table and quiet the fears he had in his head around moving forward. If he implemented Pricing Value for these legacy tradesmen, he could help them maximize their cash flow and insulate them against failure. By raising the value and providing a unique end-to-end solution to the number one problem that kept his tradesmen clients up at night, he could easily justify a decent price increase which meant he didn't have to fire a single one of them.

He could also now clearly see that if he failed to execute Pricing Value with the 35 legacy clients, he actually risked losing his own firm. And ironically, the fear of going under for Brad was far more powerful than the fear of re-valuing a few clients.

Sometimes, you just have to put your fear into perspective.

Table 12.1 How to Complete a Client Review

Client	Sector	Structure	Size	Lifecycle	Services	Manager	Referrals	Value	Pain Points	Solutions
Bob Builder	Trades	Sole trader	Micro	Start up	• Book-keeping • Payroll • Taxes	Partner	Low	B	• Cash flow • Pricing • Hiring and retaining staff	• Streamlining billing and collections • Predicting cash flow • Pricing review • HR systems

Identify WIIFC (What's in It for Clients)?

Imagine for a moment that one of your biggest suppliers, be it your landlord or your primary cloud accounting provider, announced today that the amount you pay was about to go up by 50 percent. Your first reaction is likely to be shock, your second a strong desire to know why, and your third would have you contemplating whether you're getting enough value to justify the increase.

That is why it is absolutely vital to involve and engage your client in the process of Pricing Value. If the overall amount goes up, even by a little bit, they are going to have exactly the same questions in their heads unless you manage the process masterfully. There is no need for you to "get a story together" or prepare a mass e-mail for your clients explaining why your prices need to go up because this is not a discussion about price, it's about value.

Consider this your chance to start over—to go back to the beginning and start the relationship off on the right foot—by taking the time to really understand what is keeping each client up at night. Pricing Value isn't about you, your practice, or the price you need to get. It's about how you can Create more Value for your clients.

Until you Create more Value, you haven't earned the right to increase your price. Said another way, your customers won't get better until you do.

Anticipate Objections

If you follow the Pricing Value process step by step, it will help minimize last minute objections which threaten to derail or delay the decision by your client. The best case scenario is that you will discover (through the process of Comprehending and Creating Value) what the deal-breakers are early on in the process, so you can address them with your client when you Communicate Value.

However, it is unrealistic to think you can pre-empt all objections. The best way to combat these is to do your homework. The harder you work, the less objections you will get. Take some time to brainstorm all the objections you think you will receive when you approach your existing clients. Then, as a team, create responses that remove or diffuse the deal-breakers and role-play delivering those so that each member on your team is comfortable.

Make a Plan to Re-value All the Affected Clients

It's now time to decide when you are going to contact each of your existing clients. If you have to implement Pricing Value for a large number of existing clients, it is best to segment them into groups and phase these conversations across 3, 6, or 12 months. Start with the clients that you have the best rapport with and with whom you honestly feel you can Create the most Value.

Many accountants have found that the best time to re-quote is 1–3 months before the financial year end. The reasons for this are:

- You have the opportunity to completely review their business needs before the new year.
- This is often the best time to Create Value in terms of cash flow and tax planning.
- Your current annual engagement is likely due for renewal around this time.

But what about clients whose increase will be substantial?

Let's go back and examine in depth what happened when Brad went through the exercise of re-valuing his legacy clients, including the 35 that he thought were lost causes.

He knew exactly what he had to do: meet with each of them face to face and go through all 6 steps (the 6 C's). However, he found it hard to get started. Whenever he planned to hit the phone and book the meetings, something "urgent" always seemed to come up to divert his attention away—like the time he needed to arrange a new supplier for printer toner cartridges.

Even though he was achieving great results with new clients, he still found himself procrastinating or avoiding having "the conversation" with existing clients. One night, as he lay awake in bed, the truth finally dawned on him. He knew that his tradesmen clients were in severe cash flow pain but he also knew they were financially illiterate. This combination was diabolical because he suspected it meant they were likely to be price sensitive even though what he was proposing could put more money in their bank accounts.

Brad turned on his nightlight, grabbed a notebook, and jotted down the beginnings of a great plan. He would show his clients, in a way that they could understand, what they were risking. He would show them that they could no longer afford to avoid their underlying cash flow problem. He grabbed his copy of Financial Foreplay off his bookshelf and after a quick review of Chapter 1, he drew a quick picture of exactly what cash flow looked like using the simple example of a bathtub—something he knew would make perfect sense to his tradesmen clients (refer to Figure 12.1). Instead of trying to teach them accounting, he created a highly visual, old-brain friendly way to show a tradesmen why his cash flow situation looked at lot more like a shower, than a bathtub… and the specific actions he needed to take to fix the leaky plumbing!

To his surprise, these crucial conversations went far better than he could have ever anticipated. His clients in the building trade may not have understood the accounting intricacies of cash flow, but they understood

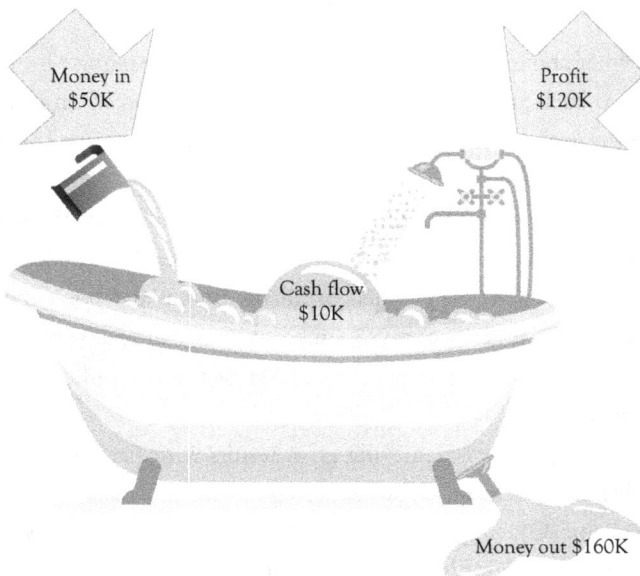

Figure 12.1 Visual Depiction of Cash Flow

his simple visual depiction—the leaking bathtub. He captured their undivided attention masterfully by nailing their key pain point on the head, proposing a solution that would cure it, and then proving beyond a shadow of a doubt that he could deliver on what he promised.

When he communicated the amount they would need to invest in order to acquire the cure, only a few of them hesitated. But because Brad had done his homework and quantified the cost of the cash flow pain in dollars to each client per month, none of them were willing to de-prior-itize the solutions that Brad had put together in his highest priced (that is, A package) option. They knew and acknowledged that something had to change in their businesses, and they also felt in their gut that Brad was the right man to help stop the leaks.

Despite his fear, Brad didn't lose a single tradesman and each of them confidently agreed to the new engagement based on more value. He did lose about 10 percent of his other legacy clients, but they were killing his cash flow and they were also the most resistant to change. They told him they could find a better deal with another accountant. Brad did not argue; he simply wished them well. In truth, he was glad to see them go.

Twelve months later, Brad reviewed his figures. By implementing Pric-ing Value across the board, he had increased his turnover by 27 percent and his cash flow by a massive 132 percent! His overall client numbers stayed roughly the same and his team members were confidently creating even more value for their clients.

As Brad discovered, the biggest battle with price increases was NOT his existing clients refusing to accept them, but rather conquering his own fear and understanding that he first needed to create more value. That evening, as Brad switched off his bedside light, he reflected on the year just past. His clients appreciated the value and impact that he added to their business, and were happy to pay him a premium. He also had more resources to reinvest in developing his team. Not only did effectiveness and impact increase, but staff retention also skyrocketed because each team member felt challenged and appreciated.

CHAPTER 13

How to Increase Revenue Quality in Your Firm

Cash flow is the lifeblood of a business, and your accounting practice is no exception. The quicker you get paid, the better it is for your cash flow, which is why many accountants have made the move to billing their clients up front in monthly installments, rather than invoicing annually after the work has been completed.

Here's one accountant's journey from debtor chaos to cash flow nirvana.

Mid-afternoon, Arun enjoyed nothing more than a pot of Earl Grey tea, served from antique Royal Worcester porcelain. It gave him the lift he needed to push through to the day's end. Arun had acquired his appreciation of the finer things in life as a partner in a prominent mid-tier accounting firm. As well as a secretary who prepared his tea, he used to enjoy the support of a large finance team, that managed the day-to-day drudgery of invoicing clients, collecting payments, and maintaining a healthy cash flow. With a decent bank overdraft to cover any contingencies, life was good in the mid-tier firm. But when Arun struck out on his own, things changed dramatically.

He, like many others before him, decided to offer his clients 30 days to pay. After all, that was how it had always been done. He wasn't concerned initially, but when he got very busy, invoicing often got postponed to the end of the month, or even later. Arun failed to notice the warning signs; he just assumed the money would keep flowing in, the way it always had previously. Then a handful of clients let their payments blow out to 90 days, and Arun suddenly realized he had major problem on his hands. The average time to collect debtors had stretched out to 65 days and his WIP was out of hand.

Arun took immediate and decisive action. He instructed his team to finalize tasks as quickly as possible, and send the invoices out straight away. As a result of this directive, his team started prioritizing simple jobs they knew they could do quickly and get paid for promptly. This led to a nasty backlog of complex and year end jobs.

As the middle of each month loomed, Arun grew nervous. Would he have enough cash to pay wages, or would he need to dip into the reserves he had set aside to meet his sales tax obligations? His practice was spiraling out of control and he needed to find practical solutions to fix his cash flow crisis properly, once and for all.

Wisely, Arun sought the advice of a few trusted colleagues. "Simple!" they told him. "Set up a direct debit system, and bill your clients each month, up front." Arun nodded. Direct debit really did sound like the answer to his prayers.

But Arun immediately began to second-guess himself. His last attempt at decisive action had actually made matters much worse. Besides, he still had a few niggling questions he could not yet answer. Therefore, he jotted them down:

- What technology should I use to make the billing and credit control seamless?
- At what point during the financial year should I start the monthly billing?
- What should I do about clients who are in the middle of their year when they switch to monthly billing?
- What's in it for the clients if they move to monthly billing by direct debit?
- What will happen to those clients who (for whatever reason) refuse to switch to monthly billing?

"This time," he decided, "I'll answer these questions before I begin. That way there won't be any unforeseen consequences."

Perhaps you find yourself in the exact same situation as Arun with most of your existing clients? Or maybe, you just have a few legacy clients who are paying after the work has been done? Regardless of which position you find yourself in, before you make the switch to monthly billing by direct debit, it makes sense to look at both the benefits (to you and your clients) and the implementation issues inherent in making the shift.

Why Bill in Monthly Installments by Direct Debit?

As Arun quickly discovered, making the shift to up-front monthly installments by direct debit (or credit card) has many benefits for you the accountant:

1. It puts you in control of your billing, workflow, and collections as opposed to the situation you find yourself in right now where you are reliant on clients to bring their records in on time.
2. Cash inflows are smoothed out over the year rather than being concentrated around seasonal peaks such as the financial year end.
3. Gives you greater certainty—ensures you always have a base level of cash coming in every month to cover your fixed monthly outgoings such as wages, rent, subscriptions, and so on.
4. WIP is effectively reduced to almost zero, eliminating the need to find dedicated internal resources to manage credit control.
5. Strong monthly recurring revenue (MRR) drives up the value of your accountancy practice because it is highly scalable and predictable.

But remember, if you are Pricing Value, you also need to know what the Economic Value is in the eyes of your clients. Some of the more obvious advantages are:

- Spreading their payments to you out over the year (possibly even in line with their own cash flow cycle, as opposed to a standard 1/12 of the total each month) minimizes the impact on their cash flow.
- Paying by direct debit means they don't need to remember to trigger the payment to you.
- Visibility of agreed payment for the whole year eliminates nasty unexpected billing surprises at the end of the year.
- You are responsible to deliver the value agreed upon each month—leads to regular, proactive advice, focus, and accountability to ensure each client receives real value.

Once Arun made the switch to up-front monthly installments, he found there was a massive unexpected benefit. Now that his clients were paying monthly, they had an expectation that they would speak to him or someone from the team much more regularly. Some accountants might see this as a problem, but for Arun, it proved to be a boon. Instead of only contacting the client when they needed records or data at year end, they were now speaking to clients every month and getting much closer to them in terms of knowledge, trust, and rapport. They now had a deeper, more intimate understanding of what was really going on in each business and the owners were much more likely to consult with them when there were important decisions to be made.

The closer they got to their clients, the more likely they were to stay with Arun's firm and upsell themselves to additional solutions. And on special occasions—like when one of his oldest clients won a lucrative contract to develop software for the federal government and Arun's team was able to help her negotiate a working capital facility to fund the 300 percent growth—he even broke out the Royal Worcester to celebrate the auspicious occasion in the boardroom with the entire team.

When to Commence Monthly Installments

It's up to you to decide on which month is best to start billing your clients up front. The first step of course is to first arrive at the agreed upon price. If that is specified as a monthly amount, you can commence billing immediately. If the agreed price is an annual amount, you must then agree to how the installments will be broken down. The easiest method, of course, is always 1/12 per month. However, the easiest method is not always the best one.

If you have clients who are reluctant to move to regular up-front installments, one of the best strategies that you can employ is to match the payments to their cash flow cycle—this has the benefit of Creating Value for your client as they will pay more when they are financially able to do so, and less when cash flow is tight. Focusing on your client's needs and cash flow cycle (and not your own) demonstrates that you are serious about Creating Value for them.

Please note that from a Pricing Value perspective, your clients' pain points and the value they need to derive from working with you are not static. Ideally, you should be meeting with clients each quarter to revisit the value that has been delivered and explore how the engagement will be modified to Create Value moving forward. The more proactive you are at reviewing the engagement and value delivered with clients each quarter, the more successful you will be at managing the tangible and intangible aspects of value.

Can Technology Help You?

Technology can make a huge difference if you want to make a smooth transition to up-front monthly billing.

There are many solutions that integrate with the major cloud accounting packages and allow you to take payment via credit card. But not all clients want to pay via credit card. Ideally it makes sense to offer both direct debit and credit card payment facilities.

What If Clients Balk at Up-front Monthly Billing?

As Arun discovered, there will always be a small handful of clients who don't want to move to monthly billing or use an automated payment system. If you find yourself in this scenario, it's incumbent upon you to create more Economic Value so that the switch becomes a non-issue. Also, you must clearly demonstrate that the change to the rules of engagement—how you will be working more closely with them each month to deliver value based on what is important to them—is structured to ensure that they can afford to pay each month. Focus on the specifics of what you will be doing in the next few months to cure pain (or achieve their dream) and deliver the value they seek.

If you have specific clients who simply refuse to switch, you may want to consider:

- Alternative payment options where payment is made manually on the first of each month (with a 3–5 percent interest penalty if it is made late).
- A small discount (2–3 percent) for using the automated billing service.
- Specifically constructing the payment schedule around the cash flow cycle of the client so it is easier for them to pay.

- A firm-wide policy where you are ready to walk away from work unless it is billed monthly via direct debit.
- A value-added incentive (turnaround time, specific team member assigned to their engagement, and so on) if they move to direct debit.

CHAPTER 14

Creating Good Pricing Habits and Mindsets

It is really tempting to think of Pricing Value as a methodology that you simply learn and then "implement" in your firm. After all, there are a set of rules and sequential steps—as an accountant it seems perfectly logical to just expect to follow them to your desired result. It's what you have done in the past. You learned new skills or knowledge and you put them to use in your practice almost immediately.

The only problem with such a plan, as it pertains to this new beast called Pricing Value, is that it is overly simplistic and naïve.

It ignores the monumental impact of all the bad habits, inefficient systems, negative beliefs, lagging indicators, and mindset that you brought into this journey with you. And if you are still billing some clients (new or existing) based on hourly rates or fixed pricing, then you cannot ignore the indelible impression of these legacy factors on your firm, team, and results.

For a moment, cast your mind back to Chapter 4 where we explored the fatal consequences that 13 highly capable and experienced men suffered because they were unable to drop the equipment and tools that weren't working and seek new methods to escape the fire. Holding on to all that useless equipment and learning made it impossible for them to think and do what they needed to do in order to survive. The situation you now find yourself in is eerily similar.

It begs the question: "What are the poleaxes, shovels, and backpacks you're currently trying to run with in order to implement Pricing Value?"

What existing habits, systems, measurements, compensation schemes, training, mindsets, and models of behavior do you need to ditch in order for your firm to survive and prosper?

And perhaps more importantly, "if you don't put them down, what hope do you have of implementing Pricing Value with any degree of success?"

The training, mindset, skills, approaches, and experience that got you to where you are now are not going to get you to where you need to be. Unfortunately, you are not starting your Pricing Value journey fresh from ground zero with no prior experience or legacy systems. The situation you find yourself in is very different from, for example, learning a brand new language where every new word you are taught is a brand new piece of knowledge in your mind that didn't exist before. This sort of additive learning is fairly straightforward and easy to accomplish because you are not constrained by old ways of doing things.

Remember, the skills, mindset, internal processes, and philosophy behind hourly based rates and fixed packages are vastly different from those required to excel in Pricing Value. Failure to do a proper 180 degree turn from what you have done before is the biggest risk factor you face in implementing it properly. And this is where it becomes tricky as you must essentially unlearn (or drop) the training, culture, skills, systems, measurement tools, compensation schemes, and mindsets that are at odds with Pricing Value. And yes, that includes a whole lot of things such as timesheets, metrics that are important to you but not your client, partner compensation schemes, and so on.

The most formidable problem with learning a new approach like Pricing Value is actually unlearning what you have been doing up until now.

Why the Bigger Problem Is Unlearning

Most people mistakenly associate learning with the experience of adding new knowledge and skills. However, sometimes the most useful learning of all is to first unlearn something that is false, no longer true, incomplete, or just plain unhelpful. In every aspect of your practice, you are operating with mental models, systems, culture, and approaches that have become outdated or obsolete due to digital disruption—and that is true from lead generation to sales, operations, customer service and delivery, finance, technology, and leadership. What worked even two years ago isn't considered best practice today and the pace of change is ferocious and unrelenting. To embrace the new logic of Value Creation and Capture under Pricing Value, you must first unlearn the old one(s). Unfortunately, neuroscience has proven that it is not easy or expeditious to unlearn mindsets and habits that no longer serve you.

Unlearning is a conscious, deliberate choice. This is of course made more difficult when the new learning directly contradicts your current understanding. Confirmation bias causes you to search for, interpret, favor, and recall information in a way that confirms your current or pre-existing beliefs, mindsets, or hypotheses. It basically makes it next to impossible to let go of what you have always done.

You must first step completely out of the old model in order to see more clearly and then intentionally select a new alternative model, perspective, or paradigm. In the words of Alfred Korzybski, a Polish philosopher and scientist who is best remembered for his theory of general semantics, "the map is not the territory." In essence what he is saying is that your perception of the world is not entirely objective but rather heavily influenced by what your mind interprets and how you describe it in language. No matter how detailed your map is, it is only a snapshot of the terrain or your subjective interpretation of what the territory really looks like.

Therefore, the biggest challenge in unlearning is that most of the assumptions or beliefs that you have about pricing are highly subjective and below the level of consciousness. Until now, they have probably never really been examined or challenged by you in any meaningful way. You initially learned (or were taught in your first accounting job) that cost-based methods and time tracking were the established convention and you accepted that. You now use those assumptions, training, and experience (without conscious thought) to operate, and you will likely cling vehemently to their veracity, even though fairly simple arguments, like the ones presented in this book, easily render them impotent, incorrect, and unhelpful.

Let's take a look at how the initial adoption of hourly-rates or fixed pricing and all the other legacy systems (like timesheets for instance) that go along with it, are playing out in your firm.

In the accounting industry, thinking and language are permeated by data (numbers), the past, deadlines, billable hours, profitability, and services. The world around you, however, has become pre-occupied with digital disruption, timely access to insights (not data), removing friction to funding, value creation, predicting the future, deeper more holistic relationships, and collaboration. Most of your colleagues have not kept up—they still see the world as linear, financial, and transactional. It is evident from the way they operate and market themselves. Clients and services are still segmented into buckets (primarily financial) even though your clients want holistic collaboration with you across all aspects of their business and wealth planning for the future.

Most accountants target and run campaigns that push generic service-based messages out to clients who are then forced through channels as opposed to engaging with each client one-on-one as a human being. Clients are shuffled, as if on a conveyor belt in a manufacturing firm, through a process that delivers an undifferentiated service instead of recognizing that the journey (from the client's perspective) is non-linear and more akin to co-creation.

So it begs the question "how do you go about teaching an old dog new tricks?"

Learning New Tricks When You're an Old Dog

The process of unlearning is relatively straightforward—according to behavioral psychology there are three main components.

1. Recognition

   The first step is to of course recognize that the old mental model, mindset, or habit is no longer true, relevant, or effective. This is particularly challenging because the outdated ways of thinking and behaving are often deeply ingrained or below the level of consciousness. Most may not even recognize that the existing model or paradigm is outdated. If you have built your practice on the mastery of these old pricing models, letting go can trigger many fears and insecurities such as the loss of control, authority, or even your sense of self.

   Once you have recognized that the old models or learning are no longer relevant or effective, the only pathway forward is to step outside so that you can gain new and better perspectives. One easy way to do this is to join a discussion group, forum, or mastermind

CREATING GOOD PRICING HABITS AND MINDSETS 173

where likeminded professionals gather to explore possibilities and discuss the veracity of various alternatives. Having support to break free from old outdated ways of thinking is paramount because it is very easy to slip back into what you have always known and done. Old habits are hard to break.

2. Create or adopt new model

It is only after you have recognized that the old way isn't working and stepped out of that model or paradigm that you can truly begin to explore, create, or learn new ways of better achieving your goals. At first, you may even find that you still have a tendency to see the new model through the rose colored lens of the old paradigm. There may be things about the new model that really appeal to you but yet you still feel compelled to hang on to aspects of the old way of doing things. This is very normal. Take your time and be patient with yourself.

Dedicate time and energy to fully exploring all aspects of the new model and ensure that you fully understand all the implications before diving in and committing.

The most likely scenarios where you will see this showing up in the context of Pricing Value is in the way you approach and work with your clients, how you track and measure the success of your practice, or partner compensation. For instance, many accountants who embark on Pricing Value, make the fatal mistake of hanging on to timesheets to track efficiency. The notion of timesheets and the desire to measure efficiency are deeply embedded in the practice of billing by hourly rates or fixed packages (as both are based on cost plus methodology).

However, timesheets are not required for the purpose of setting your price or managing your internal operations. Let's take a quick look at the four principal excuses accountants give for hanging on to timesheets and how these have effectively been refuted by the new model for Pricing Value.

The first relates to a belief that timesheets are required for pricing. For all the reasons outlined in this book, time is in fact irrelevant to setting your price based on value. The subjective theory of value alone proves that labor (time spent) is meaningless in the context of value. Your costs to complete a tax return do not determine the price, let alone the value that your client will ascribe to it. Always remember, clients buy outcomes not the number of hours it takes you to do the work.

The second reason relates to the need to use timesheet data to determine efficiency. From a back-of-house perspective, timesheets exist purely to manage efficiency but efficiency is no longer a relevant metric under this new model of pricing. You are now in the relationship business: It is possible to be efficient with things but the goal is now to be effective with your clients. You can have the most efficient practice in the world but that does not mean your clients will value what you do or your firm will be worth more than the firm down the street. Efficiency also does not guarantee that you are Creating or Capturing Value. The difference in value between a firm that Prices Value and one that does not, will primarily come down to effectiveness in customer service and the ability to Comprehend, Create, Capture, and Communicate Value. Remember, your clients only care about the value that you deliver for them—effectiveness is far more relevant than efficiency, and it will often be measured or judged in ways that have nothing to do with the number of hours it took to complete a project. Effectiveness is a measure of what is important (or of value) to your client. As a result, it is now more important that your firm delivers a certain amount of value by a specified time for instance, as opposed to worrying about how much time and materials went into the project.

The third objection relates to the notion that timesheets are vital for project management. There is a glaring problem with this assertion in that it assumes you can use time as a proxy to measure how complete or valuable a piece of work/solution is to your client. On the topic of completeness, timesheets always look backwards, whereas project management is solely concerned with predicting and managing the future. Unfortunately, by the time you see an issue on a timesheet, it has already occurred and thus can no longer be managed. Perhaps Ed Kless and Ron Baker said it best when they remarked "measuring the completeness of your projects by hours billed is akin to listening for the smoke detector to determine when your cookies are done. The alarm only goes off when it's too late." In practice, project management is now a vital tool for your firm, and when implemented properly, it will replace the need for timesheets. It all comes down to creating a comprehensive list of issues and measurements and then using those to determine the likelihood that the value/impact will be delivered by the date promised to the client.

And finally, many accountants cling to the timesheet based on the false conviction that they are needed to determine profit per job, customer, or group. Unfortunately, profit can be very deceiving. It is of course a function of revenue (real cash if you have sold something) minus costs (based on subjective cost allocations). What this means is that your costs are not *real cash costs* in a dollar and cents way—they are just arbitrary allocations that can differ widely depending upon the method you choose to calculate them. For example, the cost that you estimate for a particular accounting service could be either $97 or $138 depending upon the assumptions and cost accounting method that you use. Each time you sell that particular service, you do not pay someone $97 or $138 for the privilege of doing it. Furthermore, if you don't sell that service today, you don't save $97 or $138 in cash. And worse, if you are wrong in your estimation of the cost at $138, you may choose to turn down an engagement because it is seen as "unprofitable" (even though it may not be on a cash basis) and that decision could actually be detrimental to your cash flow.

Costs, while expressed as a dollar figure, are not *real cash costs*—at best they are simply an approximation. The fundamental problem with the profit calculation is that it is often expressed as a dollar figure, which gives the illusion that real money is changing hands. If you run your firm and make decisions purely based on profit per employee, per hour, or per service, you run the risk of making bad decisions because you could easily allocate your precious capacity to low value clients or make decisions that harm your cash flow. Unfortunately, for all of the reasons just explained, the profit calculation creates meaningless numbers that you treat as gospel and it forces mathematical relationships that simply don't exist. That is why margins and timesheets can never help you predict the need for additional capacity, determine whether you've left money (i.e., value) on the table, or show you how to improve the performance of your team.

3. Ingrain new mindsets, models, and habits

Finally, you must deeply ingrain the new learning much in the same way that a new habit is formed or a bad habit is broken. Dr. Maxwell Maltz, the author of Psycho Cybernetics who was featured in Chapters 2 and 3, discovered that it takes a *minimum* of 21 days to embed a new habit. Other more recent research by Phillippa Lally at the University of London[1] suggests that it may take a minimum of 2 months. Regardless of whether the minimum time is 21 or 62 days, the fact remains that it takes concerted effort every day for a long period of time to embed a new habit and make it stick. Unfortunately, humans are prone to falling back into the old way(s) of thinking and doing. It's therefore crucial to put strong systems, structure, and support in place when Pricing Value to ensure the new way of thinking and doing becomes accepted and deeply ingrained in your firm.

For example, even something as simple as language can become vital to keeping everyone on track. Where team members are drawn off track and into discussions about profitability and efficiency on a project, it is imperative that you as the leader of the firm to emphasize and reinforce the key drivers and leading indicators that are important to the goal of Creating and Capturing Value.

The good news is that brain science and neuroplasticity have demonstrated that the brain continues to learn, expand, and develop throughout life, which means it is never too late to rewire your brain by actively practicing unlearning. In fact, the act of unlearning and re-learning trains your brain and accelerates your ability to make shifts much more quickly. You can visually experience this process at work in an experiment by

---

[1] Lally, P., C.H. Van Jaarsveld, H.W. Potts, and J. Wardle. 2010. "How are Habits Formed: Modelling Habit Formation in the Real World." *European Journal of Social Psychology* 40, no. 6, pp. 998–1009. https://doi.org/10.1002/ejsp.674https://onlinelibrary.wiley.com/doi/abs/10.1002/ejsp.674

Destin Sandler in a video titled the "backwards bicycle."[2] The video can easily be found on Google with a simple search.

As you watch, you will see and experience the unlearning process first hand. It is fascinating to note that the process of unlearning is not linear at all. One moment Sandler cannot ride the bike at all and then suddenly, he can. It is as if a switch is suddenly flipped in his brain when the new neural pathways he was building connect and begin to run smoothly, allowing him to ride the bike.

The most important point to note from this great video and also from the material that has been covered in this book is that it is completely unreasonable to expect to solve the problems that you have in your practice with the thinking and behaviors that created them in the first place. At this time of unprecedented change and disruption in the industry, flexible and agile thinking is actually more important than any technology that is thrown at you. High tech is not the solution. High touch is.

Your mindset, habits, and models of the world across many aspects of your practice may no longer be relevant or correct. In order to move forward and Price Value, it's not as simple as learning some new models, strategies, steps, or processes and putting them into practice. You must first let go and unlearn ALL of the training, skills, systems, measurement tools, compensation schemes, and mindsets that are at odds with Pricing Value.

The key to moving forward is to first identify where your thoughts, mindsets, and firm models are in a rut?

You now have some important knowledge about how vital Pricing Value actually is to your survival, but you are still in the early days of gaining a deeper understanding around how to make the shift effectively. Perhaps you've already identified where you have some rigidity or blockers in your thinking about different aspects of your practice? Maybe you've taken a few steps toward implementing but found that distractions are constantly creeping in and making it impossible to complete the unlearning and re-learning process?

---

[2] Destin Sadler. "The Backwards Brain Bicycle: Un-Doing Understanding." https://ed.ted.com/featured/bf2mRAfC

Right now, you are looking at your practice with a bias, whether you realize it or not. Just as it took Sadler eight months of practice to learn how to ride his backwards bicycle, it's going to take time, practice, and accountability to shift your practice to Pricing Value. Unfortunately, as an adult your brain is not as elastic (in terms of unlearning and re-learning) as a small child but it can be done. The key to your success lies in what you do now.

As you learned in Chapter 3, the only thing left for you to do is to tie the knot in the rope (i.e., commit) and start climbing. The future of your practice depends on your ability to redefine what it means to be an "accountant" by stepping up and delivering a whole lot more value to your clients. If you are ready to begin the process of unlearning and you are open to having some fun while re-designing your practice, creating more value for your clients, capturing more of that value for your firm, AND being held accountable to your goals, then please join us as part of the Pricing Value training and mentoring program.

About the Author

Rhondalynn Korolak is the founder of businest® and Make the SHIFT™. Rhondalynn qualified as a lawyer and chartered accountant in Calgary, Alberta, Canada, and practiced in the oil and gas taxation niche with PWC and Macleod Dixon. After immigrating to Australia, she practiced as a business coach specializing in cash flow management and created businest®—which won The App You SHOULD be Using at Accountex in 2016 and was named in the Top 10 new apps in the world by Intuit QuickBooks. Rhondalynn now works exclusively with accountants as an advisory trainer, keynote speaker, and pricing value expert. She's distilled the secrets to success and produced a step-by-step process that accountants can apply to attract more high-value clients and build a thriving advisory practice.

Rhondalynn is the best-selling author of *On The Shoulders of Giants*, *Financial Foreplay*, and *Sales Seduction*. In the USA, she has appeared on/in CNN, Bnet/CBS, Intuit QuickBooks, Yahoo, Accountex, Accounting WEB, and Insightful Accountant. In Australia, she has appeared on/in Channel 7, Channel 9, Kochie's Business Builders, 3AW, MYOB, Intuit QuickBooks, *Institute of Professional Accountants Magazine*, *Accountants Daily*, *Dynamic Business*, *Business Spectator*, and *Australian Retailer*.

Index

OTHER TITLES IN THE MANAGERIAL ACCOUNTING COLLECTION

Kenneth A. Merchant, University of Southern California, Editor

- *Revenue Management: A Path to Increased Profits, Second Edition* by Ronald J. Huefner
- *Cents of Mission: Using Cost Management and Control to Accomplish Your Goal* by Dale R. Geiger
- *Sustainability Reporting: Getting Started, Second Edition* by Gwendolen B. White
- *Lies, Damned Lies, and Cost Accounting: How Capacity Management Enables Improved Cost and Cash Flow Management* by Reginald Tomas Lee, Sr.
- *Strategic Management Accounting: Delivering Value in a Changing Business Environment Through Integrated Reporting* by Sean Stein Smith
- *Management Accounting in Support of Strategy: How Management Accounting Can Aid the Strategic Management Process* by Graham S. Pitcher

Announcing the Business Expert Press Digital Library

Concise e-books business students need for classroom and research

This book can also be purchased in an e-book collection by your library as

- a one-time purchase,
- that is owned forever,
- allows for simultaneous readers,
- has no restrictions on printing, and
- can be downloaded as PDFs from within the library community.

Our digital library collections are a great solution to beat the rising cost of textbooks. E-books can be loaded into their course management systems or onto students' e-book readers.

The **Business Expert Press** digital libraries are very affordable, with no obligation to buy in future years. For more information, please visit **www.businessexpertpress.com/librarians**. To set up a trial in the United States, please email **sales@businessexpertpress.com**.